MAXI
THE ULTIMATE RACING EXPERIENCE

MAXI

THE ULTIMATE RACING EXPERIENCE

by PREBEN NYELAND

with Jill Bobrow and Dana Jinkins

Concepts Publishing, Inc.

For Irene

First Edition

Library of Congress Cataloging-in-Publication Data

Nyeland, Preben 1943 -
Maxi...The Ultimate Racing Experience

1. Yachts and yachting. 2. Yacht racing. I. Title.
GV813.N97 1990
797.1'4--cd20

Concepts Publishing Inc.
P.O. Box 1066
Bridge Street Marketplace
Waitsfield, Vermont 05673
Telephone: 802 496-5580
Telefax: 802 496-5581
Telex: 4949444 Books

Distributed in the United States and Canada by:
W.W. Norton & Company, Inc.
500 Fifth Avenue, New York, NY 10110

ISBN 0-393-03340-6

Printed in Singapore by Palace Press

Acknowledgements

Author/Photographer	Preben Nyeland
Editorial Director	Jill Bobrow
Creative Director	Dana Jinkins
Associate Designer	Bonnie Atwater
Editor	Alessandro Vitelli
Associate Editor	Janet Hubbard-Brown
Contributing Writers	Roger Vaughan
	Peter Bateman
	Eric Hall
	Alessandro Vitelli
Editorial Assistant	Cheryl Rousseau
Darkroom Technician	Robert Jinkins
Additional Photographers	
Beken of Cowes Inc.	Roger Lean-Vercoe
Craig Davis	Giles Martin-Raget
Daniel Forster	Neil Rabinowitz
Lucian Frank	P. Schiller
Guy Gurney	Rick Tomlinson
Dana Jinkins	Yoichi Yabe

Many people have helped me during my 20 months of gathering information and photographing the 30 yachts of the Maxi Class.

I would like to thank my wife Irene and our son Marc for their support, help and understanding, and Jill Bobrow and Dana Jinkins of Concepts Publishing, Inc. for accepting my proposal for this book. Dana selected all the photographs, from more than 4,600 taken, and I agree with her every choice. Jill did a magnificent job, by not only editing, but also correcting grammatical errors and my Danish-English syntax.

My thanks also to Soren Tang Jensen for his trust and support, Serena and Stuart Alexander who gave me and my family shelter several times in England, and my further thanks to Sue and John Colebrook for housing me in their beautiful house in New Zealand.

From the first meeting Bill Whitehouse-Vaux was more than ready to supply me with introductions and to go through the history of the ICAYA. I should also like to express my thanks for the help and information given by the owners, skippers and crew from all the yachts. My thanks as well to the designers, who kindly supplied all the drawings.

For the chapter on construction, a special thanks to Baltic Yachts for supplying the very illustrative drawings. More special thanks go out to my fellow photographers including; Chris, Dana, Daniel, Gilles, Guy, Rick, Roger and Yoichi with whom I so often have worked throughout the world.

Finally, to all my friends and colleagues, a special appreciation for their support, encouragement and understanding.   Preben Nyeland

* Editor's Note: Maxi boats frequently change names and owners. Changes have been noted up to Spring 1990.

Contents

8 **Introductions**

9 **Point/Counterpoint**
Opinions on Maxi racing

12 **History**
Windward Passage I and Great Britain II

14 **Designers**
Bruce Farr & Russell Bowler • German Frers • Ron Holland • Martin Francis • Jacques Fauroux • Gilles Vaton • David Pedrick • Rob Humphreys • Guy Dumas • Javier Visiers

20 **Anatomy of a Maxi**
Construction Methods • Building a Modern Maxi • Rigging • Sail Development • Electronics

30 **ICAYA** (International Class 'A' Yacht Association)
Course Map • History • The Crew • The ICAYA Boats • Race Results

130 **Whitbread Round the World Race**
Course Map • History • What it Takes • The Whitbread Boats • Race Results

224 **Comparative Chart of Maxi Statistics**

Maxi

"Maxi" is the term to describe the biggest yachts
in rating, length, width, sail area, etc., eligible under the
International Offshore Rule of the International Yacht Racing Union.

Introductions

We met Danish yachting journalist Preben Nyeland in Guernsey several years ago when we were all covering a Swan Regatta. Preben was familiar with our books, *Classic Yacht Interiors* and *The World's Most Extraordinary Yachts*, and approached us about producing the definitive book on Maxi Racing Boats.

It seems that some people confuse mega with maxi, so defining maxi was the first step — Maxis are boats that race under the maximum IOR rule. There are inshore maxis that race around the buoys and offshore maxis that participate in long-distance racing. Our book includes all maxis.

The inshore racers, proud of their Corinthian status, shun sponsorship, and have formed their own governing body, the International Class 'A' Yacht Association (ICAYA) to protect their preferences. These owners and crews form a proud brotherhood, and their presence enlivens regattas whenever they appear.

The growing interest in long-distance racing, epitomized by the Whitbread Round The World Race (WRTWR), represents the other aspect of maxi yachts. Boats and crews are relentlessly pushed to the limit for weeks at a time, testing the endurance of both. Sponsorship has caused this branch of maxi racers to capture the public's imagination. People can turn on ESPN, the cable sports TV network, and watch the crew of *Merit* trimming sails in the Southern Ocean!

Preben conscientiously followed the ICAYA Maxi circuit around San Francisco, St. Thomas, Newport, Mallorca, Sardinia and St. Tropez. He also traveled to the starts or finishes of various legs of the 1989/90 WRTWR in Southampton, Auckland, and Fort Lauderdale, obtaining all the necessary information, photographs, and profiles of owners, skippers and designers.

Concepts Publishing ended up with five-thousand photos to edit, yacht specifications to verify and numerous taped interviews for our editor, Sandro Vitelli, to decipher (despite the handicap of having to make out a Dane conferring with a Frenchman in a windy cockpit with noisy repairs all around). The result is a colorful, exciting portfolio of the world's largest racing boats.

Whether inshore or offshore, maxis are for the stouthearted to own and sail, but their beauty and power belong to all sailors. This book then, is for all who dream of sailing fast. Maxis are the ultimate racing experience!

Jill Bobrow and Dana Jinkins

I feel privileged to have been asked to contribute an Introduction to the ICAYA section of this book into which Preben Nyeland has put so many years of research, travelling extensively before beginning to write the book. He and the editors have prepared a wonderful format that the reader will certainly enjoy.

I began my sailing/racing career some 63 years ago. Quite apart from the obvious fact that in that time I have seen many changes in the type of yachts, construction methods, accessories of all kinds, crews, racing rules and the men who implemented them as well as types of racing — one thing remains paramount — the sea and wind are constant. Constant, that is, in the fact that they can never be taken for granted or assumed to be the same. Always keeping that fact in mind, it is amazing that in a few short years in this post-space age, such radical changes have been made in exotic construction materials, electronic navigational aids, and racing programs that could not have been visualized just a few short years ago.

The most heartening thing is that far from becoming less proficient because of their reliance on modern techniques and instruments, the crews of today are certainly more proficient than the crews of the sailing ships in the "great days of sailing." Without such crews, it would not be possible for a modern maxi to be raced at its upper limits, and it is not too much to say that without such crews, ICAYA could never have developed in the short space of ten years.

If the last 15 years are a testament to change, then the future of yacht racing is sure to be exciting. A short time after ICAYA was in existence, the Association suggested that the America's Cup Trophy might someday be sailed for in larger yachts than the International Twelve Meter Class, leading to the evolution of the larger type of International Class 'A' yachts racing today. These yachts are basically fitted for inshore racing only, but at a very high level. Some regard this as a retrograde step, but it is the kind of racing that owners of these yachts like and is not much different from the type of I.Y.R.U. and U.S.Y.R.U. racing that has taken place over the years.

A final word. Maxi yacht racing, whether ICAYA or otherwise, offers the most exciting racing experience at the present time.

William Whitehouse-Vaux

It was during our stopover with *Flyer* in Auckland in the 1981/82 Whitbread Round The World Race that I first met Preben Nyeland. He struck me as a very friendly and well-informed yachting sports writer who, apart from all the technological aspects, also understood that yacht racing is the ultimate test of the bond between crew and skipper.

I am honored that he has asked me to write an introduction to this book and I wish him all good fortune in his future endeavors.

Clare Francis said, "Modern yachts must be the most complex pieces of sporting equipment yet thought of." And how right she was — especially the modern maxi class yachts (offshore as well as inshore), where technological development has made enormous strides, breaking through existing frontiers in the search for speed. The lighter and stronger materials for hull, mast, rigging, sails and the use of advanced electronics, better clothing and new safety devices are evidence of an evolution that reflects all the way down from the maxis to small racing craft and cruising boats.

It's not just the sophistication of these yachts that make them exciting. As there are often more than twenty crew members on board, it is team effort that is all important. There are times when the adrenaline flows fast during rough weather conditions. In races like the Whitbread, the adrenaline is often flowing fast!

I applaud the recent formation of the Offshore Maxi Owners Association led by Pierre Fehlmann and its aims to develop a series of events for the ocean-racing maxis in the three-year cycle between Whitbread Round The World Races. This can only produce much greater public awareness in a sport that should be seen matching crews against the elements.

To see the beautifully sculptured lines of *Windward Passage*, *Kialoa*, *Steinlager 2*, and *Fisher & Paykel* cutting an effortless swathe through the seas is like poetry to all who sail.

Conny van Rietschoten

Dissension in the Ranks:
How an Amateur Sport (Formerly Professional) Became (Partially) Professional Again

by Alessandro Vitelli

Perspective is often the first victim of any divergence of opinions among dedicated, enthusiastic men. This book's format, within the context of current maxi boat developments, reflects the fundamental rifts that have evolved between offshore and round-the-buoys races; sponsored and privately financed yachts and yacht races; and professional versus amateur sailors.

It might be well for us to remember that racing large yachts started as an almost exclusively professional sport. Wealthy owners hired professional captains and crews, and watched the races from shore or from the comfort of their steam yachts, betting heavily on the outcome. Professional captains such as the Americans Charlie Barr and "Hank" Haff, and the British Captain Sycamore made a good living racing the huge racing schooners and sloops of the late 1900's for their owners.

Also worthy of attention are some additional historical notes. The first time the J-Class sloops, the early maxis if you will, were sailed in the America's Cup challenge in 1930, they were essentially stripped-out racing machines, with no accommodations at all below decks, as had been their immediate predecessors, the huge extreme gaff-rigged sloops such as *Reliance*.

Arguably, the first amateur maxi crew ever was found on *Endeavour* during the 1934 America's Cup races, hastily signed on at the last minute after T.O.M. Sopwith's professional hands unsuccessfully went on strike for higher wages and were laid off. Interestingly, it was then felt that the previous challenge's yachts were not built in the proper spirit of yachting, and all the 1934 and 1937 J-boats carried complete, if spartan, accommodations below. With the advent of the J-boats the first amateur skippers — wealthy yachtsmen such as Harold S. Vanderbilt and T.O.M. Sopwith who actually commanded their yachts personally — came on the yachting scene.

Finally, while no teabag logo appeared on the sails of Sir Thomas Lipton's *Shamrocks*, it can safely be assumed that the publicity he gained from his five challenges for the America's Cup did not hurt business.

Professionals vs amateurs; private ownership vs syndicates (and sponsors); stripped-out inshore racers vs proper ocean-going yachts. In the 1980's, with the surge of public interest in the offshore racing exemplified by the Whitbread Round the World Race, and with the organization and growth of the International Class 'A' Yacht Association (ICAYA,) these conflicts have resurfaced, once again dividing sailors who fundamentally share the same passion.

Perspective demands that we remember that yacht racing, of which maxi racing must be considered the most magnificent manifestation, is undertaken for the beauty, the romance, the competition, in short, for the sport of it, whether experienced or vicarious, private or professional. Any activity as demanding and complex as the design, construction, and campaigning of a maxi, involving as it does talent from such a diversity of disciplines, cannot be limited to any one set of restrictions. ICAYA, an avowedly "self-defense organization," was set up by amateur yachtsmen who love racing at the top, but whose business interests give them limited time to devote to their passion. That it might have allowed "unhealthy hybrids" (as their maxis have been called) to develop is almost beside the point — their owners have chosen to race 'round the buoys; the boats are the result of that choice. The increased popularity of yacht racing has made the Whitbread maxis more visible, thus more interesting to sponsors. But before the amateurs condemn professionalism and sponsors' money they should consider the tremendous evolution in yacht technology and safety, not to mention the quality of the racing, made possible by that money.

There are no losers, only winners, in the sea-going debate; let these maxi sailors, winners all, speak for themselves...

Point/Counterpoint

"Just as yachting begins to attract a wider audience, those involved in racing maxi yachts seem intent on allowing the discord between private ownership and sponsorship to divide this most prestigious section of the sport."
Cornelis van Rietschoten, owner/skipper of *Flyer*, twice winner of the Whitbread Round the World Race

"Maxi yacht racing, whether ICAYA or otherwise, offers the most exciting racing experience until the present time."
William Whitehouse-Vaux, owner of *Mistress Quickly*, ICAYA Vice-President, Eastern Hemisphere

"I don't think [I will go into ICAYA racing] because you need a lot of money, a sponsor is not permitted, and I think it is a completely stupid way to utilize a maxi... to race for 25 miles and come back is nothing. A big boat like this, the right utilization is a big race... If you want to race a 25-mile race sail a J-24!"
Giorgio Falck, owner/skipper of *Gatorade*

"The Whitbread goes too far as far as I'm concerned. I still have a business to run and I cannot take that much time off. I get a certain enjoyment from racing but I would not get the same enjoyment spending months at sea. That to me is not the same. But now we're at the other side of the coin where we're spending [only] several hours racing."
Huey Long, owner of *Ondine VII*

"The owners of maxis such as Merit, Milene, or Rothmans should be encouraged to participate in regattas other than the now prevalent Olympic triangle day races. We might then see a revival of interest [among the maxis] in races such as the Fastnet, the Malta Race, the Bermuda Race, etc."
Gilles Vaton, designer of *Milene*

"This can only produce much greater public interest and awareness in a sport that should be seen matching crews against the elements as much as their rivals, and not merely measuring the depth of an owner's pocket."
Cornelis van Rietschoten

"Belmont Finland was a good opportunity to start racing maxis and not put in that much money because you don't have a chance to win the race (the Whitbread Round the World race) when you are a first-time skipper. You should not spend that much money on a race like this if you do not have a chance to win."
Harry Harkimo, skipper of *Belmont Finland II*

"I like Jim Kilroy's remark: someone asked him if this isn't a rich man's sport, and he said 'No it isn't: there's one rich man on board and there's 25 poor men and they enjoy it more than the rich man does!'"
William I. Koch, owner of *Matador*

"We race for fun, we race for our own satisfaction, and we do it against competitors that we respect."
John B. Kilroy, owner of *Kialoa VI*, ICAYA Vice-President, Western Hemisphere

"We got a sponsor [early on]. The project was always approached with the objective that if we couldn't get all the money there was no point because the boats that did have all the money were going to beat you."
Grant Dalton, skipper of *Fisher & Paykel*

"Today, media interest, particularly from television, has encouraged sponsors to take command of entire [sailing] projects, just as they have been doing in motor sports for many years."
Cornelis van Rietschoten

"I would say that, up until the Fifties, a racing driver would be a guy from a rich family most of the time... It was gentlemen's racing, because they were wealthy people. They could afford to buy a Bugatti, they could afford to buy an Alfa Romeo... But then you start coming to the [era of] semiprofessional or professional racing drivers... And then the teams started saying, I need a really good driver, a professional guy, so I know I'm going to win.
"That was a transition... [Then] sponsors really started becoming involved, when Grand Prix racing became open to sponsorship. Suddenly, there was a great development in racing, because it opened up opportunities for thousands of drivers all over the world. Once real money was involved, the technology accelerated quickly. More teams, more people, more different categories in the sport."
Emerson Fittipaldi, 1972 and 1974 Formula One World Champion, 1989 Indianapolis winner *

"I was disenchanted with the way international racing was going. It was becoming obvious that victory was only available to those who could find massive funding, even in those days [racing] was becoming too expensive for an ordinary yachtsman."
Bob Salmon, skipper of *Liverpool Enterprise*

"The Class 'A' Maxi Association (ICAYA) has consistently refused to allow any form of sponsorship... The group, made up of a few owners [who can personally afford owning and campaigning maxis], has resulted in unhealthy hybrids - yachts once intended to race across oceans, or a least compete in the great classic ocean races, now compete only 'around the cans.' Indeed, these owners visibly recoil at any suggestion of racing offshore."
Cornelis van Rietschoten

"Frankly, my preference has always been for long-distance racing, ocean racing, not around the buoys. Around the buoys racing is fine, it's exciting, but it is not what my background is... For me it's kind of fun to do the long-distance race, it shows how good your crew and your boat are in all kinds of conditions over a long period of time."
Huey Long

"I also think ICAYA is losing some of its original intent: meeting at interesting places and having fun racing together from one place to another. The maxi yachts are confined to an Olympic triangle course without having the passage races and feeder races.
"I believe those big boats should not confine themselves to match races or Olympic triangles. Day races and Olympic triangles are misdirected. Maxis should have races like the Fastnet, minimum, [requiring] knowledge of meteorology, navigation... you live with the ocean, you live with the elements, choose options according to the winds, that is very gratifying."
Albert Mirlesse, owner of *Milene V*

"If inshore racing is the great attraction, there is no better competition than in the America's Cup, and the inspired rule insisting that the owner or his representative be on board these new yachts gives the backers a chance to be carried into battle too, not left to watch from a distance."
Cornelis van Rietschoten

"I think that the inshore maxis will become closer in spirit to the 12-meter... it is regrettable that stripped out IOR maxis were not chosen for the next America's Cup; it would have simplified everything and provided some good even racing."
Gilles Vaton, designer of Milene

"The demise of day-racers due to the new 75-foot America's Cup class of yachts capturing the limelight , will leave the way clear for the real maxi yachts to take center stage once more, as well as attract the levels sponsorship that will increase competition and the circuit of races."
Cornelis van Rietschoten

"The sport has changed, become a profession, unfortunately, which is very bad. People have been very prone to come into the sport and pay to have the best talent on board, and that's very much contrary to what I have done all my life which was to make it an amateur sport. Today you see people not even interested in helming the boat, or navigating, or doing anything in the boat except to sit there and hope that the boat wins and pay for whatever it takes to make the boat win."
Huey Long

"The crew is the key part of winning a race. You are taking a group of very interesting young people and merging them together, working with them, training them, setting up the rules of how you run your boat... and you're doing it for fun."
John B. Kilroy

"The most heartening thing is that, far from becoming less proficient because of their reliance on modern techniques and instruments the crews of today, even though some are highly specialized, almost certainly are more proficient than the crews of sailing ships and larger sailing yachts in the great days of sailing. Without such crews it would not be possible for a modern maxi racing yacht to be raced at its upper limits."
William Whitehouse-Vaux

"It's the most technical, the most skilled group, the world's best racing."
John B. Kilroy

"I am interested in sailing because it is one of the sports that really brings you close to nature and forces you to muster all your talents in order to use the wind and the sea to your advantage."
George Coumantaros, owner of Boomerang

"I feel also more sailors in the world would like to go cruising, with family, friends, live on board, enjoy sailing, and sometimes, not all the time, also go for a good race."
Herbert Dahm, owner of Inspiration

"And sailing can be a goddess of fun or a goddess of destruction."
John B. Kilroy

"I consider the fact that my [ICAYA maxi] Longobarda, the Whitbread maxis, and the new America's Cup yachts are all almost exactly the same length and very similar in their other dimensions an interesting coincidence."
Gianni Varasi, owner of Longobarda

"Maybe I'll write a book for my children, so they can have a record of how nuts their father's been."
Ludde Ingval, skipper of Union Bank of Finland

"In my 63 years of racing I have seen many changes in the types of yachts sailed, construction methods, accessories of all kinds, crews, racing rules and the men who implemented them, and types of racing. One thing remains paramount, the seas and wind are constant, constant, that is, in that they can never be taken for granted and can never be assumed to be the same. Keeping that fact in mind it is a matter of amazement that in a few short years in this post-space age such radical changes have been made in exotic construction materials, electronic navigational aids, and racing programs that could not have been visualized such a short time ago, and that all these are now well-known."
William Whitehouse-Vaux

Point/Counterpoint

Windward Passage I and Great Britain II

The undisputed grandparents of the modern IOR maxis, whether built to withstand the rigors of the Whitbread Round the World Race or the tight inshore racing typical of the ICAYA yachts, are two perennial favorites, *Windward Passage I* and *Great Britain II*, both designed by Alan Gurney.

Windward Passage I was built for Robert F. Johnson under a tent in an empty lot in Freeport, Grand Bahama. According to John Rumsey, the project manager at the time, she was built for the express purpose of beating all the records of Johnson's previous boat, *Ticonderoga*. Johnson was the owner of the Georgia-Pacific Lumber Company, so the boat was built of wood. Her floors and structural members were fir and the hull was triple-planked Sitka spruce covered with epoxy.

Rumsey unloaded the first shipment of lumber for the boat in November, 1967. *Windward Passage* was launched just one year later and within a month had won her first race, the Miami-to-Palm Beach event. In 1969 she won the Palm Beach race again, and took top honors in the Miami/Nassau race, and the Los Angeles-to-Honolulu "Transpac," setting new records for both races. Johnson died in 1969, but his sons, Mark and Fritz, continued to campaign the yacht. In 1971 she broke her own Transpac record with a time that stood until 1977 when *Merlin* snatched the prize.

Bill Johnson of Atlanta (no relation) bought *Windward Passage* in the early 1980's and put a new rig on the boat. He was rewarded for his efforts with wins at the S.O.R.C. and the maxi series that year in Hawaii. She also took line honors in the PanAm Clipper Cup the same year. Her 1982 Miami-Montego Bay elapsed time of three days, three hours still stood as a record as of April 1989.

The owner since 1985, Australian Rod Muir, took the yacht to Tim Gurr's yard in New Zealand for a complete refit. The yacht was stripped to the bare hull. The old "wet" stern was redesigned. The keel was redesigned to hold 14 tons of lead with room for 850 gallons of fuel. Her floors were replaced with an aluminum space frame and new bulkheads made of plywood over foam were installed. A new composite deck and cockpit replaced the original.

Great Britain II was build by D. Kelsall and launched in the early summer of 1973 from Ramsgate. She was christened by Her Royal Highness Princess Anne, and sponsored by "Union" Jack Hayward for the first Whitbread Round The World Race in 1973/74.

Chay Blyth was her skipper and *GB II*, as she has since been affectionately called, was the first yacht back in Portsmouth after 144 days 10 hours 43 minutes 44 seconds.

In 1975 *Great Britain II* made another circumnavigation of the globe. This time it was a one-stop race sponsored by the *Financial Times*. The co-skippers were Mike Gill and Roy Mullender and again *GB II* set a new record by beating the clipper ship *Patriarch*'s London-Sydney-London long-standing record of 69 days for each leg, which had stood since 1869/1870.

In 1977 the second Whitbread took place and *Great Britain II* was again at the starting line, this time with Robert James as the skipper. Though she finished back in Portsmouth 16 hours behind *Heath's Condor* she again set a new record by cutting almost 10 days off her own four-year old time.

GB II functioned as a charter boat over the next two years, until a young Scandinavian woman, Cecilia Unger, bought the yacht with the intent of racing her in the upcoming Whitbread. Participation in a round the world race is expensive, so when a sponsor was found they brought along their own skipper, Chay Blyth. *GB II* had a major refit, and changed her rig from ketch to sloop. At the end of the third Whitbread Race, under the name *United Friendly*, she was 12 hours faster than her first race eight years earlier.

When Unger owned the yacht, she also did some tall ship racing, training youngsters. In 1985/86 the yacht was in the hands of Bob Salmon who only managed to procure a sponsor one day before the start of the fourth Whitbread Race. Racing under the name *Norsk Data* she was more than five days faster than four years previously.

A yacht that has raced five times around the globe should be tired, but *GB II* did not show her age when she again was to be found at the starting line for the 1989/90 Whitbread Race, her fifth attempt under her fourth name, as she was now called *With Integrity* and under the command of Andrew Coghill. Whatever her current name, she is still known to all as *GB II*, sharing with *Windward Passage I* the grandparenthood to the high tech flock of today's maxis.

A. *Under full sail,* Windward Passage I.
B. Windward Passage I.
C. GB II *as* With Integrity D. *...as* Norsk Data E. *...as* GB II
F. *...as* United Friendly.

D.

C.

GUY GURNEY

E.

BEKEN OF COWES LTD.

B.

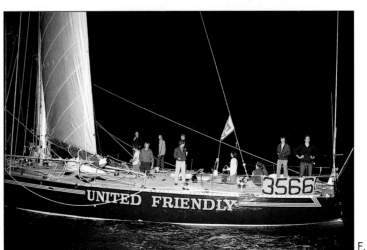

F.

Windward Passage I & Great Britain II

Designers

SUZY STOUT

SUZY STOUT

Bruce Farr and Russell Bowler
Annapolis, Maryland

Bruce Farr's name is practically synonymous with maxi designs. For the 1989/90 Whitbread, Bruce Farr & Associates, Inc. designed seven of the 14 maxis competing: *Belmont Finland II*, *Fisher & Paykel*, *Gatorade*, *Liverpool Enterprise*, *Merit*, *The Card*, and *Steinlager 2*. They have designed the ICAYA maxis, *Hispania* and *Longobardo*.

Farr started dinghy sailing at a very early age and at 12, designed and built his first boat. At 21, he opened his design office in Auckland, New Zealand and entered the very competitive 18-footer scene. He designed cruising boats, and added Quarter, Half, Three Quarter and One Ton IOR boats to his portfolio with World Championships in each of those classes to his successes.

Russell Bowler joined the firm permanently in 1980 after having worked with Farr on a consulting basis since 1975. The association began much earlier however, as the two competed against each other on the race course in dinghies of their own design. Through the late sixties, Bowler won national and world dinghy titles with his own designs.

Bowler, who holds a degree in Civil Engineering, pioneered the use of light weight FRP (Fiber Reinforced Plastic) sandwich construction and its application to high performance racing boats. His construction techniques led to highly improved strength to weight ratios. Bowler's design and engineering research keeps Bruce Farr and Associates, Inc. at the forefront of yachting developments.

Farr and Bowler moved their design business from New Zealand to Annapolis in 1981. They felt the move placed them nearer to the center of the yachting world with easy access to Europe and in touch with the traditional yachting of the United States' eastern seaboard. The Annapolis office maintains a staff of 11 with seven highly skilled designers using the latest in computer software and technology for their work.

In 1989, Farr designs had many successes to their credit: One Ton Cup, 50-foot Yacht Association World Cup, Champagne Mumm's Admiral's Cup, and in the maxi world — (ICAYA) Maxi World Championships: *Longobarda* took 1st overall (with fewer than half the points of her next closest competitor); in the 1989/90 WRTWR — three of the leading boats were *Steinlager 2*, *Merit* and *Fisher & Paykell*.

Bruce Farr and Associates, Inc. were involved with New Zealand's first America's Cup Challenge in 1987, developing the first and only fiberglass 12-meter for that event. They were also responsible for the overall concept and engineering design of the much-publicized *New Zealand*, Mercury Bay's 1988 America's Cup challenge giant.

At the age of 41, Bruce Farr has achieved dominance in the international sailboat design field at a time when it is more competitive than ever. Editors at *Yachting Magazine* recently wrote, "At a time when most yacht designers seem to specialize in something, Bruce Farr excels at everything."

German Frers
Buenos Aires, Argentina

Frers' early racing success began when he was seven, racing dinghies, and then Lightnings. While still in high school, Frers started working as a draftsman in his father's design office. Now 49-years-old, he has accumulated an enviable record with his many racing designs; a glance at the list of maxis actively racing reveals just how successful he has become in this particular form of yacht racing.

Frers designed his first boat in 1958, when he was 17. He later moved to New York, where he spent three years working at Sparkman & Stephens, at that time the leading American yacht design firm. He then started his own office in New York before returning to Buenos Aires in 1970. There he took charge of the design firm founded in 1928 by his father.

His first designs after his return to Argentina, *Matrero* in 1971 and *Recluta* in 1973, established his reputation with their successes in the Admiral's Cup. Since then approximately 400 designs have been created by Frers, including *Scaramouche, Noryema, Ragamuffin, Congere, Volcano, Flyer,* and *Bumble Bee*. His credits in the roster of maxi yachts consist of 25 designs, among them *Boomerang, Emeraude, Kialoa V, Ondine VII, Matador, Il Moro di Venezia I, II,* and *III,* the ex-*Windward Passage II,* and *Martela O.F.*

Boats and sailing have been in Ron Holland's blood since he was a small boy in his native New Zealand. He designed his first boat at the age of nineteen — a 27-footer which he describes as "basically a cruiser, but fast!" His first job was as an apprentice in a yacht-building yard in Auckland, but he left to compete in the Sydney-Hobart Race and then to cruise in the Pacific.

In 1973, *Eyghthene*, designed and built by him in Florida, won the U.S. Quarter Ton championship and then the World Championship in Torquay, England. Soon afterwards he designed *Golden Apple* which performed outstandingly in the One Ton Cup, and firmly established his design philosophy.

Ron Holland
Cork, Ireland

Further commissions and racing successes followed, including victories in the Admiral's Cup, Fastnet, Sydney-Hobart, Bermuda Race, SORC and many other international races. Many of his designs, such as *Imp, Regardless, Morning Cloud,* and maxi designs *Condor* and *Kialoa* became household names among sailors. Holland's cruising boats incorporate many of the lessons learned from his racing achievements, earning him commissions both from individuals and from production yacht builders.

"The success of my racing designs was the springboard of my organization's move into creating the new breed of big sailing yachts."

Holland feels that his breadth of experience, not just of design, but of the sea and sailing, is responsible for his success as a designer. From an early age he sailed all types of craft in all types of conditions; in 1970 he journeyed from San Francisco to Australia via the Pacific Islands in a 35-footer without an engine. The time spent as a boat building apprentice enabled him to acquire knowledge of the techniques of boat building production and made him determined to obtain the very best from a wide variety of materials available today. He is aware of the practical implications — in terms of performance and function — of the various theoretical aspects of yacht design. As head of Ron Holland International Yacht Design, his interest in designing boats remains passionate as does his commitment to developing new and exciting ideas.

"Although most of my work these days is designing large cruising yachts, I remain involved in the racing scene. There is an intellectual challenge about it, and undoubtedly the associated research and development has beneficial spin-offs for all my yacht design projects."

About his maxi designs: "The first opportunity came with *Kialoa IV*. At the time she was the largest IOR maxi at 80 feet, and also the first to use composite Kevlar construction. She was World Champion for three years. *Condor* was a development on *Kialoa IV* and largest at 81 feet. She took the composite construction system further and was built predominantly from carbon fiber.

"*Sassy* was a small maxi at 78 feet, built specifically for the light conditions of the Great Lakes. *Lion NZ,* at 78 feet, and *Drum,* 77 feet, were designs aimed at the Whitbread Race. *NCB Ireland* takes this concept further and is a much larger design at 81 feet."

Designers

Martin Francis
Antibes, France

Martin Francis and Jacques Fauroux are the designers of *Satquote British Defender*. The objective presented to the design team was to provide a competitive boat capable of being sailed by the varied talents of the British Army, Navy and Air Force.

Martin Francis has extensive experience in designing large high performance cruising yachts. His previous experience with maxis was with the 78-foot IOR, *Speedy Gonzalez*. Fauroux's experience as a competitive sailor and his expertise in the IOR rule enhanced their collaboration.

Francis was born in 1942 in England and has lived in France for the past 12 years. He was educated at St. Christopher's School and studied Industrial Design at the Central School of Art and Design in London.

From 1967-1977 he taught Architecture and Industrial Design at the Architecture Association, Hornsey School of Art, and other schools.

During the period from 1981-1987 he created, with Peter Rice, the Paris-based engineering office, R.F.R, which is the consulting firm chosen by the French National Museum of Science and Technology at La Villette to assist in the study of domes and suspended glass facades braced by cables. They acted as consultants to I.M. Pei on the Pyramide du Grand Louvre in Paris project.

Since 1967 he has worked in collaboration with Norman Foster and is currently Director of Foster Associated, London and Managing Director of Foster France.

In the field of naval architecture his experience covers all stages of design and construction, from conception up to yard supervision and the tuning of the yacht. He has designed more than 17 boats from 55-foot sloops to 138-foot centerboard sloops and ketches. He currently has under construction a 240-foot motor yacht with a top crusing speed of 34 knots. Martin Francis is also the coordinating designer for the *Atlantic Sprinter,* a Blue Riband challange boat with a top speed of 70 knots.

Francis believes that sponsored events, together with one -design racing, will become increasingly popular and that the IOR rule will continue to lose its appeal.

Jacques Fauroux
Cannes, France

Jacques Fauroux who collaborated with Francis on *Satquote British Defender*, has an office in Cannes. Born in 1941, in France, he has a degree in Physics and is a naval architect who specializes in IOR boats and the International 'J' class. His design achievements include *Bullit* which won the Quarter Ton Cup in 1979 and 1980, *Maligawa* which won the Three Quarter Ton Cup in 1980, and *Gitana Sixty* which won the World Cup in 1986.

Gilles Vaton
Marseille, France

Gilles Vaton is the designer of *Milene V*. Thirty-seven-years-old, he is married and has three children. His sailing career began with Vaurien dinghies and 470's. His racing experiences include the 1973/74 Whitbread aboard *Kriter I,* various single-handed races between l974-76, the 1977/78 Whitbread aboard *Neptune* (first leg), and the 1980 SORC aboard *Charles Heidsieck III*. He also participated in three Fastnets, three Giraglias and a Maxi Series aboard *Coriolan*.

He started his own firm after having worked with Rouillard, Illingworth/Nicholson, and André Mauric for ten years. His designs include: *Charles Heidsieck III* (l98l); *Coriolan*, the first French maxi (l983); *Tender To*, first ever centerboard maxi; and *Champagne Charlie* (l984).

Vaton shuns publicity, and the renown of *"Charles Heidsieck"* and his other designs has happened in spite of this fact.

"For me," Vaton said, "Actual experience is of primary importance. It is one of the main tenets of my philosophy of yacht design. For instance, I think it is impossible to properly design a yacht to race around the world without having personally participated in such an event.

"It is this racing experience which has determined one of my most important design features: I strive to improve off-wind performance, but only as long as I can preserve upwind speed. But racing experience is more than just a necessity for creating racing boats. It applies to all yachts. I believe that the lessons from racing can benefit cruising...there is a lot of give-and-take between the two.

"This give-and-take also applies to different types of boats, such as monohulls v. multihulls. And for this reason I avoid limiting my work to only one type. I am currently pursuing five yacht design 'paths': IOR racers, cruising yachts (with emphasis on centerboarders), racing multihulls, cruising multihulls and motor yachts (particularly semi-planing types).

"There is a danger in both excessive specialization and too great diversification. I strongly believe that to improve, one must collaborate with other...foreign...designers and compare one's own ideas and concepts with those of others. Complacency is the trap which otherwise can catch us."

As for maxis, "In the future I believe that an obvious distinction will be necessary between the inshore maxis — which are now completely stripped of all interior accommodations — and the Whitbread maxis with their basic accommodations that are more strongly built and easier to sail off the wind for long distances, but relatively poor sailers on the wind.

"The owners of maxis such as *Merit*, *Milene*, or *Rothmans* should be encouraged to participate in regattas other than the now prevalent Olympic triangle day races. We might then see a revival of interest [for maxis] in races such as the Fastnet, the Malta Race, the Bermuda Race, etc.

"At the same time, I think that the inshore maxis will become closer in spirit to the 12-meters...it is regrettable that stripped-out IOR maxis were not chosen for the next America's Cup; it would have simplified everything and provided some good even racing."

Designers

A 1970 graduate of Webb Institute of Naval Architecture in New York, Pedrick quickly demonstrated his abilities at Sparkman and Stephens, where his design responsibilities included the early maxis, *Tempest* and *Kialoa III* as well as the successful America's Cup defenders, *Courageous* (1974) and *Enterprise* (1977). In 1977 Pedrick founded his own naval architectural and marine engineering firm, Pedrick Yacht Designs, Inc., based in Newport, Rhode Island. He designed *Clipper* (1980) and *Defender* (1982). He served as co-designer of the Twelve-Meter *Stars & Stripes* that won the Cup back from Australia in 1987. With five America's Cup campaigns, Pedrick's experience in this premier event is unmatched by any other current designer.

Pedrick has also proved himself to be one of the leading designers of high performance cruising and ocean racing yachts. Among the custom yachts that he has designed since establishing his own firm, are: the maxi racer/cruiser *Nirvana*, current holder of the Bermuda and Fastnet Race records; *Drumbeat*, an 82-foot maxi racing yacht for Alan Bond and *Sovereign*, the 83-foot maxi that won the 1989 St. Thomas and Newport maxi regattas.

Pedrick says, "*Sovereign* was designed as a dual purpose yacht. She was to be comfortable...and still be a seriously competitive racing boat...Successful integration of often-conflicting requirements is the true test of a yacht designer, and giving our clients the most for their money is a challenge that we enjoy doing well."

David R. Pedrick
Newport, Rhode Island

One of his firm's revolutionary designs is the Pedrick Whale-tail keel, designed to improve the righting movement and hydrodynamic performance of yachts. *Sovereign, Drumbeat* and several other designs now have this new keel.

"The progressive directions in which we are currently active," observes Pedrick, "include the new America's Cup class of yacht and a 100-foot sailing mega yacht with an unprecedented speed of 25 knots under power, while maintaining extraordinary sailing performance. High-performance design work is continuing in round-the-buoys maxis, with proposed projects under the new Whitbread rule. Dynamic new concepts and engineering make this a very exciting time in performance yacht design."

Rob Humphreys
Lymington, UK

Thirty-five-year-old Rob Humphreys is the designer of *Rothmans,* the all-British maxi yacht competing in the 1989/90 Whitbread Round the World Race. A Welshman by birth, he started as an industrial designer, then became a marine journalist for *Yachts and Yachting* magazine, which led to his interest in yacht design.

The quarter-tonner *Midnight Special* was the first of his designs to be turned into a full-size boat; his second major success was the half-tonner *Roller Coaster,* built in 1979, which led to subsequent design spin-offs.

Humphreys' next design achievements were two boats called *Jade,* the first of which narrowly failed to be selected for the 1983 Admiral's Cup team, but went on to beat the majority of the Admiral's Cup boats in the Fastnet. The second *Jade* was the winner of the 1985 One Ton World Championships.

It took Rob and his team of four designers four weeks to calculate the basic design of *Rothman's* hull, although the process of refining the various designs and researching the alternatives to produce a winning boat involved several months' work. He continued to work on the yacht throughout the race although the nature of his work changed from supervising measurement to optimizing the rating.

According to Humphreys, "*Rothmans* has been designed so Lawrie can push it hard. It's spartan but not dingy; in fact there is a door on the loo which is considered an absolute luxury! There are 16 bunks in total and no special cabin for the skipper — he will have to fight for a bunk along with all the others!"

Humphreys considers his main design rival to be Bruce Farr, who has eight of his designs competing in the Whitbread Race.

"Bruce Farr is the yardstick," Humphreys acknowledges, "Everyone wants to beat his boat, but the question is, which is the real Farr Boat?"

Of all the projects that Rob has tackled, he considers the *Rothmans* design challenge a coup.

Guy Ribadeau Dumas
Paris, France

Parisian Guy Dumas is the designer of *Charles Jourdan*. Born in 1951 in Versailles, Dumas is the eldest of five brothers (all of whom sail). He began sailing at age seven on a sailing canoe and on Vaurien dinghies, and continued on 420's, 505's, Stars and Dragons.

"My father had a 10-meter which my family rebuilt and on which I raced. Paris is near Cowes so that I began in R.O.R.C. races at 17 and got much experience being crew or skipper on many different racers, mostly in the Admiral's Cup. From racing our 10-meter, I developed a passion for meter boats, and crewed on Baron Bich's twelves."

When he was only 15 years old, Dumas decided to become a yacht designer and began his technical studies, so that by the age of 20 he was an important contributor in a design office and at 22 worked on a Whitbread competitor.

He has designed several famous yachts: *Credit Agricole* 1 and 3, both BOC Challenge winners; *Rucanor*, Class D winner in 1985/86 Whitbread; and *Shark 50*, a ULDB Transmed winner. His Maxi designs are *Antares, an* 82' maxi for Eric Tabarly (never built), an 80' maxi for Baron Edmond de Rothschild (never built) and *Charles Jourdan*.

Dumas thinks the evolution of maxis has been slow. "Gurney's designs (*Windward Passage I, Great Britain II*) were competitive for a long time. The Ron Holland and German Frers period didn't favor any evolution. ICAYA races will become interesting when at least five designers such as Jeppesen, Judel-Vrolijk, Farr, Reichel-Pugh, Andrieux, Humphreys, and I hope myself, will be involved."

"Among the maxis, a very interesting point is the range of displacements, from 11,000 kilos to 39,000 kilos (24,000 to 86,000 lbs). So broad a range does not exist in any of the other IOR classes. I am certain I can design an ICAYA evolution of *Charles Jourdan* at 16,000 Kg (35,000 lbs.) to be competitive with a maxi displacing 39,000 kg.

"I see this ICAYA *Charles Jourdan* with a tiller, one cockpit, and five winches: a big Admiral's Cupper. The cost with a prepreg carbon hull and complete inventory would be around $1 million U.S.

"I made this proposal to the owner Sandro Buzzi and skipper Alain Gabbay. They took the total concept as it was; the only changes were to move the chart table from forward to aft the cockpit, move the runner winches, use a heavier mast section, and install two spinnaker pole tracks instead of one.

"My objectives were to design a downwind flyer stiff enough to remain efficient upwind and reaching with a waterline length basis equal to the others. The main objective on deck and interior are lightness (simplicity) and weight concentration to reduce the significant effect of pitching moment."

Javier Visiers
Barcelona, Spain

Fortuna Extra Lights was the first Spanish ocean maxi conceived, designed and built entirely in Spain. Javier Visiers undertook a thorough study of design and materials to create the lightest boat possible, and the one most adapted to ocean racing.

Visiers was born in Madrid in 1942. He graduated from Southampton Polytechnical University (England) with a degree in naval architecture. He has designed fast cruisers and winning race boats. Visiers also designed and brought to completion the previous *Fortuna* project, and with her won important victories in the 1984 Transmed, the 1985 Discovery Race and the 1987 Caribbean Race; he took third place in the Transat 87 and took an impressive sixth place in the 1985-86 WRTWR. He sailed on board *Fortuna* in those races.

"On a personal level, as a designer, it is a challenge to build a maxi competing with the large budgets and the high level of technology of other boats and other countries.

"In Spain, we are ready for this type of design and I also feel that the first *Fortuna* broke important new ground. I hope that this maxi continues in that same direction.

"I have the idea, and I think it is reasonable to think in these terms, that a boat which is very light and stable in reaching and running conditions is easier to push to l00% of its potential. That one meter less that we have in comparison to a bigger maxi gives us a much lighter displacement. It's easier to push the boat to its limit."

The most modern materials were used to give *Fortuna* maximum solidity without reducing safety. Carbon fiber, epoxy resin and nomex assure extreme rigidity. The rudder is built entirely of pure carbon fiber and is calculated to resist surfing pressures of up to 30 knots.

"We are the lightest maxi in the entire Whitbread [however,] weighing less doesn't mean being fragile."

Designers

Anatomy of a Maxi

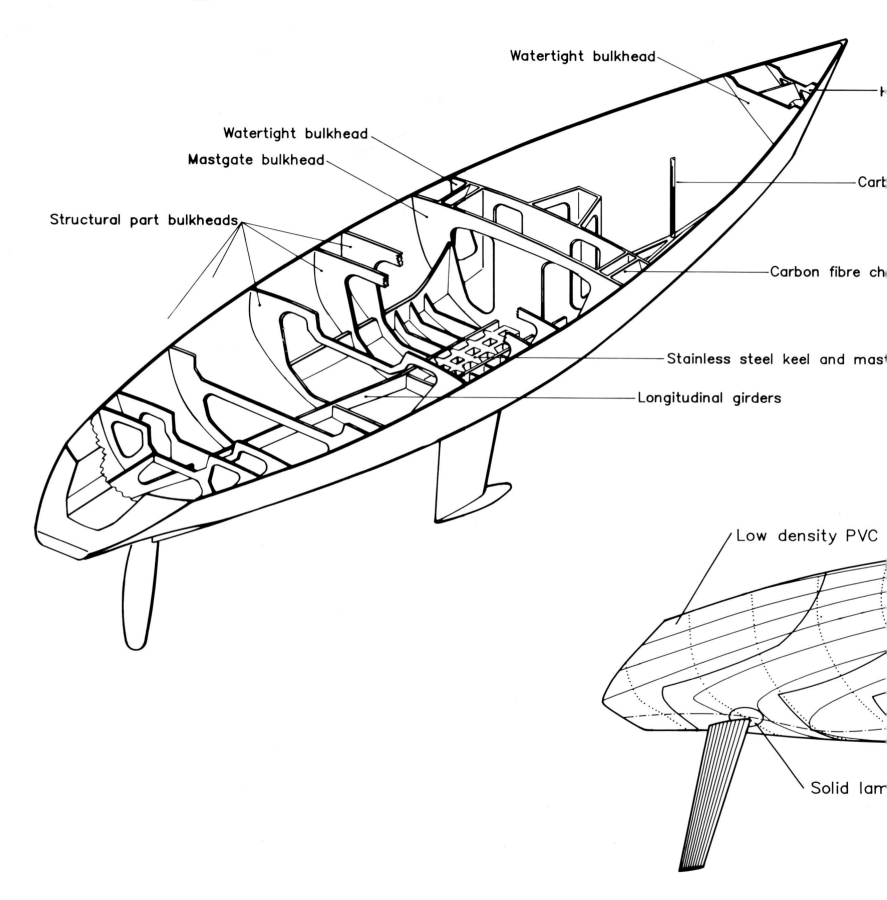

Watertight bulkhead

H

Watertight bulkhead

Mastgate bulkhead

Cart

Structural part bulkheads

Carbon fibre ch

Stainless steel keel and mas

Longitudinal girders

Low density PVC

Solid lam

chainplate

deck support

s

ment

It is human nature to create ever bigger and more daring machines, and yacht racing is no exception to this impulse. Since the turn of the century, large racing yachts have been built to class rules (The Universal Rule, which flourished between the wars and culminated in the majestic J-Boats, and the International Rule, still active today in the 12-meter and 6-meter classes, are the two best examples) but the building of maximum size yachts to a rule which would be both truly international and devised for ocean racing is a development of the last 20 years or so.

In 1969 the International Offshore Rule (IOR) was introduced and accepted on a worldwide basis. In the course of the years following its adoption, the IOR Rule has been frequently revised, to close loopholes, to eliminate inequities, and to follow the evolution of materials and techniques used for making sails and for the construction of the yachts. Needless to say, most evolutionary changes have been at the expense of the owners, and nowhere has this expense been greater than in the maxi class.

It has recently been decided by ICAYA to freeze the IOR rule for a period of five years. The cost of building a new maxi yacht has reached astronomic proportions, and yet, when subject to constant rule changes, a maxi could become outdated a year or two after launching.

The earliest construction material used in the class was wood, used for the first modern maxi yacht, *Windward Passage I*, the spiritual ancestor of today's maxis. She was designed by Alan P. Gurney and launched in 1968. Gurney also designed the other famous grandparent of the maxi class, *Great Britain II*, launched in 1973. *GB II*, as she has always been known in spite of several name changes to suit different sponsors, was built using an Airex (PVC) foam core between GRP (glass reinforced plastic) skins. These two grand old ladies are still racing: *Windward Passage* in occasional day races, while *GB II*, now named *With Integrity*, has just finished her sixth circumnavigation under her fourth name.

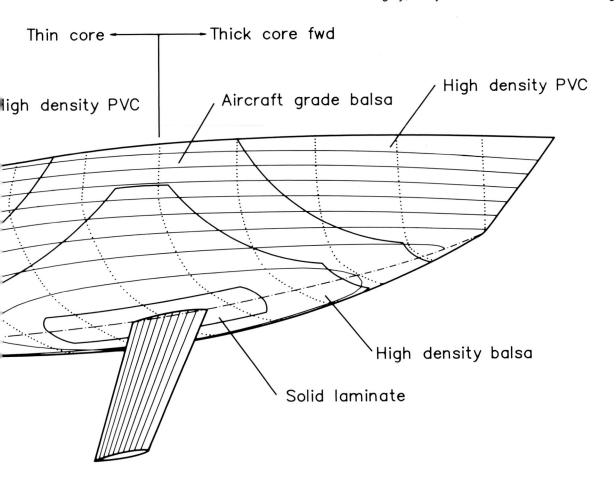

Thin core   Thick core fwd

High density PVC

High density PVC   Aircraft grade balsa

High density balsa

Solid laminate

Anatomy of a Maxi

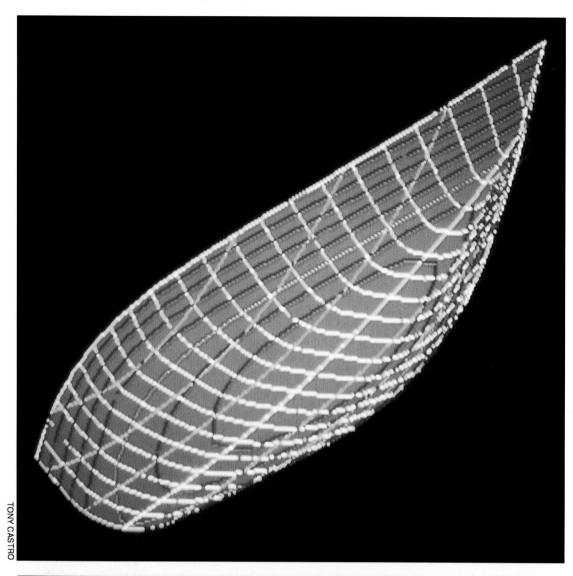

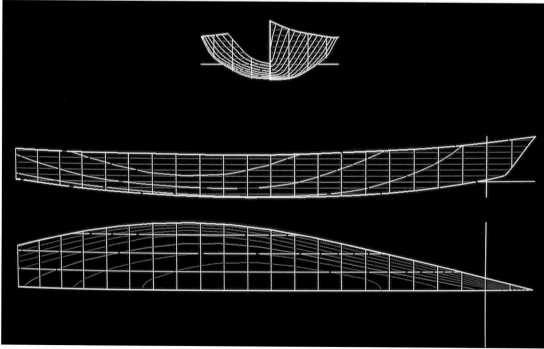

Computer generated drawings of Fazisi.

Inshore and offshore maxis were built of aluminum for several years thereafter. Aerospace experience and technology filtered down to the America's Cup 12-meters, and subsequently was picked up by designers and builders. In 1981 the 76-foot maxi yacht *Flyer* was launched at the Royal Huisman Shipyard, where a new welding technique had been developed. *Flyer*'s owner had built her to take line honors in the third Whitbread Round the World Race of 1981/82. She fulfilled his dream, and surprisingly also won on handicap as well. But the way of the future was visible in that race: Several racers were custom-built of GRP and FRP (fiberglass reinforced plastic.)

The fourth Whitbread race (1985/86) pointed out the divergence in maxi yacht construction philosophies prevalent at this period. Most inshore maxis were built of aluminum, while the offshore racers solely used composites. The early composite yachts were fitted with aluminum H-section space frames to take the tension and stresses produced by the mast, keel, engine, generator, and tanks. Two out of the six maxis competing in that Whitbread suffered delamination problems on the first leg to Cape Town, South Africa; these were rectified in time for them to continue with the rest of the fleet.

While the fourth Whitbread race was in progress, the first 12-meter yacht built of composites was launched in New Zealand, becoming a source of annoyance and anxiety to some of her future competitors.

For the 1988/89 racing season 17 maxi yachts were commissioned from ten designers. 16 were built of FRP composite construction, the hull and deck built up of Kevlar and carbon epoxy skins vacuum-bagged to PVC foam and Nomex honeycomb cores. Only one was built in aluminum, the Soviet Whitbread yacht *Fazisi*.

The current generation is doing away with the aluminum H-frame, using carbon fiber bulkheads and stringers instead, with a stainless steel plate to back up the keel. An 81-foot Whitbread maxi built to these specifications will have a hull/deck weight (exclusive of rig and ballast) of only 4,535 kilos or 9,998 pounds.

Hull weight is 2,448 kilos (5,397 lbs.), the deck is 646 kilos (1,424 lbs.), and the bulkheads and internal structure 1,441 kilos (3,177 lbs.) This makes the use of internal ballast possible, producing a very stiff yacht with a low center of gravity while removing weight and its associated stresses from the keel.

The trend to composite construction has spread to the inshore racers: Two have been built and several ICAYA members are planning new yachts. Of course, the engineering will have to take into consideration the fact that ICAYA yachts are built to race in up to 30-35 knots of wind on an Olympic course, whereas the offshore racers must take conditions as they come. There is no upper wind speed limit for them. As an added influence in the development of modern materials and techniques, the new America's Cup class will be composite boats, bringing government and corporate funds into development budgets.

The future will bring yachts where the keel will be hanging from a carbon/Kevlar structure. Composite will be the only material used.

The evolution of construction techniques exemplified by the maxis reinforces the principle that there can be no substitute for direct experience gained by sailing thousands of miles at sea. This hard-earned knowledge has enabled designers and builders to apply today's technology to the art of boat building, creating safer, faster, and ever more daring yachts.

A. Aluminum framing of Kialoa V
B. Below deck on *Windward Passage II;* the large white bulkhead is made of carbon and Kevlar
C. Counter-sunk winch aboard *Emeraude*
D. This mast on *Windward Passage II* started a trend toward lightweight spars.

C

A

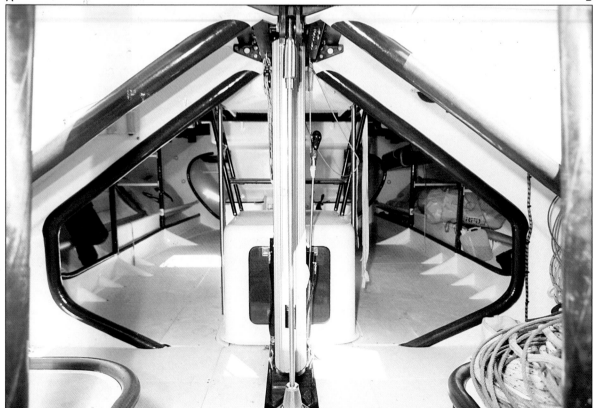

B

D

Anatomy of a Maxi

Building a Modern Maxi:

1. Lofting: All stations and halfstations are drawn up to 1:1 scale with deduction of the hull thickness, then the frames for each station are cut using the full-scale templates.
2. Building the plug: The frames are balanced and positioned on station, then covered with wood battens.
3. Surface treatment: The plug's surface is smoothed by filling and sanding, then finished with a layer of parting wax.
4. Inner laminate: Unidirectional carbon with some Kevlar.
5. Core material: Two different weights and thicknesses of balsa wood and PVC foam.
6. Outer laminate: Unidirectional carbon with some Kevlar.
7. Fairing of hull surface.
8. Plug and hull are turned over.
9. Plug is lifted out of hull.
10. Hull reinforcement and structural bulkheads are installed. Longitudinal stringers and transverse frames are built up of E-glass and carbon fiber over a high density PVC-core.
11. The deck is bonded to the hull.
12. Ring frames and bulkheads are laminated to deck.
13. Interior painting.
14. Engine and plumbing installations.
15. Electrical installations.
16. Accommodations and final interior details are finished.
17. Deck painting.
18. Deck hardware is mounted.
19. Steering systems and rudder are installed.
20. Hull painting.
21. Keel mounting.
22. Antifouling.
23. Stepping the mast and rig tuning.
24. Sea trials.
25. Ready to race.

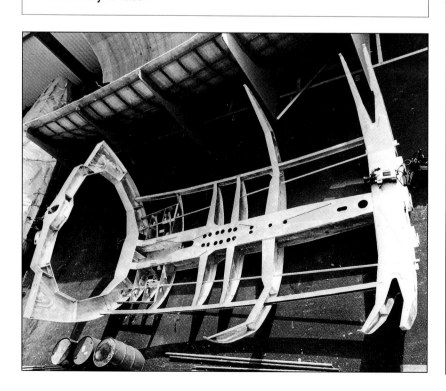

Anatomy of a Maxi

Rigging

by Eric Hall / Hall Spars

The decade of the eighties saw sweeping technological development in the maxi class. Rig development was certainly no exception.

Rig geometries evolved from relatively cumbersome and heavy three-spreader masts to elegant and ever lighter four and five-spreader rigs allowing reduced frontal areas. What you save in weight aloft, you save ten-fold in the keel. In the late eighties, fractional rigs became *de rigeur* on the IOR circuit and modern very light ketch rigs characterized the best boats in the 1989/90 Whitbread race.

Although aluminum was the dominant material through the decade, carbon masts were used as early as aboard Heath's *Condor* in the 1977/78 Whitbread. However, *Condor*'s mast broke on the first leg to Cape Town and was replaced in Monrovia by an aluminum mast. Nonetheless, by mid decade, carbon fiber took over as the material of choice for spinnaker poles and some standing rigging. (Carbon was banned for booms and masts). Carbon poles at half the weight of aluminum poles have proven tough and durable in all areas of maxi racing, enabling crews to handle huge spinnakers in rough seas. *Boomerang* on her third mast and fourth boom by the end of the decade was still using the carbon pole built for her in 1984. To date, carbon has been banned from use in IOR boats. However, with America's Cup boats using it, the ban is certain to be lifted.

Rod rigging made great strides during the eighties; much stronger and lighter than wire, rod rigging doesn't stretch, making it easier to keep the rig in trim. Early Whitbread races saw many fatigue failures in rod rigging. Because of this, companies like Navtec instituted intensive research and development programs. As a result, by 1990 Whitbread rod rigging was simpler, lighter, yet exhibited exceptional resistance to fatigue.

Galvanized wire which characterized halyard sheets and guys on early maxis has been liberally replaced with Kevlar and Spectra, resulting in tremendous weight savings.

As the stakes continue to be raised, rig development will continue to accelerate, keeping pace with rapidly advancing maxi boat technology.

CRAIG DAVIS

Sail Development

by Peter Bateman
North Sails, UK

Sail design for the inshore maxi and offshore WRTWR boats has opened new frontiers for sailmakers and the sails are surprisingly similar coming as they do from opposite sides of the racing spectrum. The link is that the development of sails keeps leapfrogging from one fleet to the other.

For years the adage, "overbuild sails for offshore and underbuild them for inshore," was adhered to. That theory has been replaced by a more sophisticated approach that has almost reversed the original theory. WRTWR sailing puts less load on the sails as they are never sheeted really hard; the loads have been analyzed, and the weights of sails and length of life reduced and increased respectively.

The nylons and Kevlar-nylon laminates such as those used on Pierre Fehlmann's *UBS Switzerland* during the 1986/87 WRTWR are sometimes successful but at other times lead to frustration; for example, when in the same race Peter Blake's mainsail tore and he dumped it into the ocean. Sails in that race suffered from the materials not being in the same stage of development — performance could be achieved, but the lifespan was unpredictable.

Parallel development by the America's Cup competitors in Newport, 1983, and more specifically in Perth, 1986, pushed the material development and construction techniques beyond what had been developed for maxis. The success was evident — sails could win races but would not necessarily survive for more than 100 hours. The K boat/catamaran America's Cup accentuated this. It was only when the 1989/90 WRTWR competitors came along that efforts were made to lengthen the life of the sails and accept a compromise on speed.

In the end, speed has not been compromised; in fact, the new development of materials and construction has meant that sails last ten times longer and perform at the peak levels.

Shapes are again top priority. Day race shape requirements are vastly different from WRTWR shapes. Some reflect the type of boats; i.e., heavier displacement, vastly higher righting moments, and the needs to point high being critical. The WRTWR boats sail at higher speeds and wider angles; they are narrow boats with minimal righting moments. These characteristics change the previous relationship between the two worlds of "maxi" boats. As both sides optimize performance to the restraints of the IOR rule, the gap will continue to widen.

Anatomy of a Maxi

Electronics

On the Round-The-World Sailboat Race it isn't the skipper that whips the crew into action—it's the computer. On board the boat that perhaps has the most advanced electronics, *Union Bank of Finland*, it isn't skipper Ludde Ingvall who dictates the activity for the experienced 15 man crew with the shout "we need more speed," he has a computer to draw attention to this fact with brutally blinking digital text! For example, if "CORR SPEED - 1.05 KN" is shown, then the helmsman knows something is wrong—he is sailing just over one knot too slowly.

So then it is just a question of trimming and steering a little more efficiently as the boat eats its way further through the 33,000 sea miles of the round-the-world sailboat race.

The computer is quite simply the most accurate and fastest navigator that any sailboat has ever had. It is the main ingredient of the electronic "food-chain" which consists of an impressive collection of navigation-aid instruments which make the navigator's little cupboard of a cabin look more like the cockpit of a Jumbo Jet. The price tag is approximately U.S. $200,000.

In all there are three different PC's to provide the computer power. Below deck in the navigation cabin a Canon-PC calculates navigation coordinates, tactics and communication, while an Apple Macintosh PC with digital display is the boat's own meteorological office. It makes local weather prognoses based on thousands of weather readings. Up on deck the crew has its own Deckman Sailmath tactical computer which provides sophisticated monitoring of the boat, just as the Canon-PC does. The Deckman is specially adapted for outdoor operation, so that the deck watch has constant access to all available data via a cable connection.

Better Equipped than an Ocean Liner

The round-the-world sailboat's small, tightly-packed navigation station actually supplies more information than the entire electronics on board an ocean liner. The instruments supply the same measurements, but the sailboat racer can additionally calculate and present the information related to the boat's own tactical capabilities. The computer's minutely detailed feedback as to whether the boat is sailing too slowly or off course, is a prime example of what this whole stack of expensive instruments can achieve. The blinking display: "CORR SPEED - 1.05 KN" does not only mean that the boat is sailing too slowly according to the electronic speed log under the keel.

The adjusted figure includes two typically computer-oriented calculations. The first is the "VMG" — value or Velocity Made Good — the optimum speed towards the next coordinate on the route. The computer knows the VMG for all sailing combinations, wind strengths and courses.

The second computer calculation included in the adjusted figure is the boat's handicap-value. Round-the-world sailboats are not all the same size and therefore compete on a handicap basis.

Thus the computer readout "CORR SPEED - 1.05 KN" tells you how well you are sailing relative to the optimum course to the next coordinate — defined by satellites — compared to the competition!

The prerequisite for all navigation and tactics is knowledge of your

1. Digital repeaters for boat and wind speed
2. Suunto Fluxgate electronic compass and repeater
3. Aneres electronic barograph
4. Ventilator
5. Furuno AD Converter. Interface between boat's own navigation instruments (compass, log etc.) and satellite navigator
6. Skanti Watch Receiver. Listens to emergency frequency
7. Sony color monitor for satellite photo and Canon PC
8. Brookes & Gatehouse echo sounder
9. Thrane & Thrane interface between fax and PC
10. Brookes & Gatehouse Main Unit for sailing instruments and Hercules sail computer
11. Sony color monitor for weather charts from Apple PC
12. Furuno digital color radar. For viewing the contents of a cloud.
13. Furuno Transit satellite navigator
14. Vanguard satellite receiver for satellite weather photos
15. AP-navigator. Decca radio direction finder
16. Furuno GPS satellite navigator
17. Nokia interface between satellite navigators and Canon PC
18. Apple Macintosh PC with Apple telefax modem. Apple Image Writer modem and Digital Board with mouse to read weather charts.
19. Pankratt 232-modem, interface between Canon-PC and

Sailmath Deckman racing computer.
20. Feedback Weather Satellite Receiver. Antenna amplifier to (14) Vanguard satellite weather photo receiver
21. Barometer
22. Chronometer with Greenwich Mean Time
23. Chronometer with local time
24. Furuno VHF-radio
25. Sony All Band Receiver
26. Canon PC with keyboard and diskette drive
27. Airphone intercom to cockpit
28. Furuno SSB radio, transmits with 400 W and reaches around the world. Transmits and receives in telephony, morse and telefax.
29. Furuno Weatherfax which continuously receives weather charts over the area where the yacht is
30. Inmarsat Comsat Telesystem. Satellite-radiophone. Primarily for telephony, but also serves telefax.
31. Handheld VHF-radios
32. Apple Macintosh fax, modem and printer. Also prints weather chart predictions.
33. Fuse board
34. Voltmeter for battery voltage

actual position, and here *Union Bank of Finland* is very well served. It finds its way across the world's oceans with the help of two different satellite navigators and two automatic radio direction finders.

The satellite navigators are fascinating, because each one is actually a very powerful mathematical calculator. The one is based on six Transit satellites, which orbit the Earth over the poles. The boat's navigator merely needs to have one of these satellites in contact to work out its position. The Transit-satellites make use of the Doppler Effect, exemplified by the change in tone of the siren of a passing emergency vehicle.

The satellite sends out recognition and a time signal at fixed time intervals. Because the satellite's orbit is known and coded into the navigator's computer, the satellite's position can be determined for each of its time signals. By using a sensitive receiver the navigator now measures the frequency changes in the signal due to the Doppler Effect. This tells the navigator which way the satellite is moving between the time signals. All that remains now is the "simple" calculation of a needle-like navigation triangle where one leg is about 500 km and the two others about 20,000 km. You are at the point of the needle!

Radio Masts out in Space

The other satellite system is called "GPS" — Global Positioning System — which will eventually be linked to 24 satellites — forming an enormous "net" around the Globe.

The GPS satellites transmit, in groups, a certain radio signal simultaneously. The navigator can now work out his position by measuring the difference between the signals.

Exactly the same navigation technique is used by the Loran and Decca Nets, in which Decca makes use of the AP-navigator— a Danish development. The Decca navigation requires the navigator to have a fairly large memory in order to house a mathematical representation of the Decca map with its "hyperbolic curves." These are the lines along which the radio signals meet when synchronized with the same time interval.

Each registered position coordinate is automatically transferred to the Canon-PC, which can thus monitor the ship's progress. The ship's own navigation instrument, log, wind direction, speed gauge, and electronic compass, are fed into a little navigation computer.

This, in turn, supplies the Canon and Deckman PC's with a series of parameters which enable them to determine the effect, for example, of ocean currents on the ship's position, and hence which sail should be set.

After a long series of sailing tests carried out before the actual race, the Canon has been fed with a large range of fixed parameters which represent each sail's potential. This is a measure of the sail's pulling power under different wind strengths, for all wind directions and in combination with other sail settings.

From a battery of sensors, both fore and aft, the PC receives important information about the boat's heel and pitch angles together with the tension in the fore and back stays. All this will be continually telling the computer — and therefore the crew— if the boat is sailing in precisely the correct trim, with the correct attitude, and also if the boat is sailing on the right course, from both a tactical and a navigational point of view.

Ten Years of Daily Weather Reports

Electronics can also make small future predictions for the navigator. Reserved for this purpose is an entire Apple Macintosh, which is programmed with all available weather maps worked out for the route during the last ten years. Each hour the navigator can retrieve from the "weather-fax" a weather map giving the prevailing high and low pressure zones. In addition, the ship is receiving satellite photos of the same type seen on the nightly TV weather forecast.

The weather maps are stored on a digital-board in the computer, enabling the navigator to "page" back and forth in the stored information to find similar sequences of events. In this way he can predict the weather conditions a few hours ahead. The weather map is displayed on one of two color TV monitors. The other monitor can be used to display satellite photos so the navigator can verify his observations.

Color radar is in fact the ship's most effective short-distance meteorologist. It can track the weather changes in the immediate vicinity, right down to distances of a few nautical miles. The crew are now able to set the course which gives the best speed.

On the Southern Ocean part of the route it isn't the odd brisk storm that gives the crew sleepless nights. They are now sailing with the Trade Winds and what they fear most is that the wind might die or turn, while their competitors sweep by, hundreds of nautical miles away to the north or south of them. This is why they don't use their sophisticated meteorological equipment to avoid stormy patches. Instead, they steer towards them!

Communication

The communications technology used is on a par with that used by the maritime profession. *Union Bank of Finland* also has satellite radio, which can communicate in digital form with the whole world.

It is an American system, Inmarsat, with a net cost of U.S. $40,000. You can call the boat from your own telephone, providing you know its call signal.

Telephone calls, telex and telefax, transmitted via the satellite, are all dumped into an array of modems in the navigation room. Telefaxes go straight into the Canon-PC's memory, from where they can be printed out if they are important.

The navigator is also in contact with the outside world — with land, with the competitors and also with inquisitive radio hams. For this, he uses his Furuno ship's radio which operates on all wavelengths on single side band (SSB), with great efficiency at long distances. Telex and fax messages can also be received this way. For short-distance communication, the navigator turns on his VHF radio and on board, the boat has two hand-held VHF radios.

What if the whole thing breaks down? Little chance of power failure — the boat has a total electricity supply of 10 kilowatts which is spread across three separate generators, with the boat's main engine generator as back-up.

Let's assume that the entire electronics gets hit by a freak wave and all the receiving aerials are swept away. We still have the compass, chronometer, sextant and nautical almanacs.

Anatomy of a Maxi

ICAYA International Class 'A' Yacht Association

The History

The International Class 'A' Yacht Association was born out of necessity. Until the middle of the 1970's there were very few racing yachts of "maxi" size, and it was rare to find more than two entered for even the most classic of ocean races.

These maximum racing yachts, or "maxis" as they are now known, were considerably larger than International Twelve Meter yachts, yet it was difficult to obtain hardware such as winches and other deck fittings. They were treated unfairly under the IOR Rule probably because they were not represented in the international forum at all. As a class or group, they had no voice. Because there were so few, no special arrangements were made for them at the various regattas.

William Whitehouse-Vaux, ICAYA Vice-president/Eastern Hemisphere noted: "There is no reason that there should have been [special arrangements] really, other than the sheer size of the boats. But if you were given a berth which was difficult to get to, you had a great deal of difficulty getting your sails on and off, things like that.

"So we really got together in the first place as a kind of self-defense organization. ICAYA was founded on August 6th, 1979, at Cowes Week. When it first started, there were very few real so-called maxi boats sailing. There was *Kialoa*, *Windward Passage*, *Ondine* and *Mistress Quickly*. I'd met Jim Kilroy in 1978 in Hong Kong and for want of competition we made a rough program of which event we would both go to, so at last we'd have a boat to race against. This was before 'A' Class came into being. About a year later *Condor* came along."

That week at Cowes, a meeting was called to discuss the maxi issue. Those present were Baron Edmund de Rothschild, owner of *Gitana*; John B. Kilroy, owner of *Kialoa*, Enrico Recchi, owner of *Benbow*; and William Whitehouse-Vaux, owner of *Mistress Quickly*. They elected the officers at that very first meeting: Edmund de Rothschild, President; Jim Kilroy, Vice-President of the Western Hemisphere and Whitehouse-Vaux became Vice-President of the Eastern Hemisphere and Class Captain. Francois Carn of the Yacht Club de France was elected Honorary Secretary.

According to Whitehouse-Vaux, "The first objectives of the Association were (and are) the encouragement of amateur yacht racing, sailing, and the organization and holding of Corinthian sailing matches, races, regattas, and competitions for sailing yachts holding valid Rating Certificates between 60-70 feet IOR measurement. Furthermore, yacht racing was to be governed by the rules of the International Yacht Racing Union, as amended by the racing rules of the Association. As both *Benbow* and *Gitana* were below the minimum rating specified, they were grandfathered."

All the original members are still active. King Juan Carlos of Spain and the Aga Khan are honorary members as was the late Herbert Von Karajan. Some members such as Harold Cudmore, Bruce Kendall, and Peter Bateman are brought in as technical advisors.

When ICAYA started, all the members were involved in ocean racing. A program was developed to include the SORC and races in the Caribbean or Europe, depending on what events were going on. The ICAYA schedule was arranged to avoid conflict with the classic ocean races, such as the Bermuda Race, the Fastnet and the Sidney-Hobart. Two or three regattas expressly for the maxis were also included in the schedule. The championships were held every other year as it was considered too problematic to move the boats between Europe and America frequently.

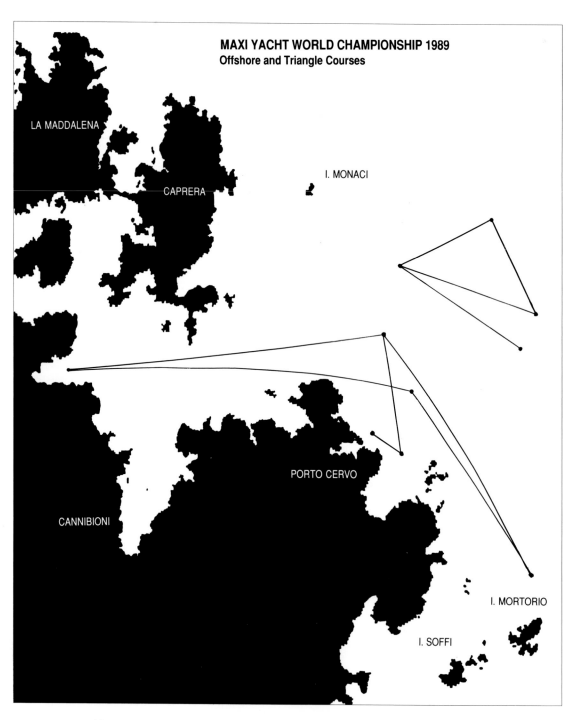

MAXI YACHT WORLD CHAMPIONSHIP 1989
Offshore and Triangle Courses

LA MADDALENA

CAPRERA

I. MONACI

PORTO CERVO

CANNIBIONI

I. MORTORIO

I. SOFFI

ICAYA

The Rules

Since its founding, the class grew to the point where it was considered necessary to have a permanent office in Europe. Under an agreement with the Aga Khan, ICAYA retained Gianfranco Alberini (who also runs the Yacht Club Costa Smeralda) as Secretary General who would be responsible for organizing and handling all ICAYA business, promotion, and public relations.

The association caters to all types of yachts rating between 60-70 feet IOR, but racing under IYRU rules. All yachts belonging to ICAYA are by definition "maxi" yachts, but not all maxi yachts are International Class `A' Association Yachts.

The by-laws of the association have recently been revised, and the championship occurs annually. The increased size of the fleet permits this change in scheduling. The format of the races have evolved as well. Match racing was introduced, and the emphasis has shifted increasingly to inshore racing. The maxis, previously pure ocean racers, assumed their present form.

Gianfranco Alberini, Secretary General of ICAYA says:

"We also noted the changes in the way the boats are raced. There is more involvement in technology and sophistication than in the past, a change that has been observable not only in the maxis, but in all the IOR classes... They are all pure 'racing machine' boats...no more cruising. It is the same in the maxis; the newest boat this year, *Longobarda*, has little to do with the original *Gitana* or some of the maxis of that vintage from when the association was founded, not only in terms of technology, but as a concept."

Whitehouse-Vaux echoes this observation:

"Between *Kialoa III* and *Mistress Quickly* and the very up-to- date modern boats, you get a very good idea of the development. In [the olden] days we had proper cabins, proper berths, galleys and so on. Now...they're virtually stripped out, in some cases completely stripped out. Galleys have become module galleys...you can put them in for passages...there are no proper berths, no refrigeration...

"However, it should be realized that there is a very strong Cruising/Racing Division in the Association whose owners do not wish to have such extreme types of yachts and who wish to have more cruising accommodation and facilities for long-distance racing."

Alberini observes that the homogeneity of the maxis can present problems when trying to apply rules which cover a wide range of boat types and sizes, "We are at a very delicate point with respect to the evolution of the rating rule. The purpose of the ORC (Ocean Racing Council) is to introduce changes and revise the rules for the benefit of the entire IOR fleet, from the smallest yachts to the maxis. So it's sometimes difficult for them when they introduce a change [based on an average size], to also satisfy the extremes. So ICAYA being at one extreme of the rating rules, we are looking very carefully at what is going on with the changes. There is a lot of concern among the members that rule variances may affect the class. If someone is building a maxi yacht, which is quite expensive, it is possible that the boat may become obsolete because of the technology, but certainly not because of the rules. There is the possibility that as a class we may decide to freeze the rules for a certain period [of time], to protect the owners from obsolescence due to rule changes."

NEIL RABINOWITZ

A

A. Big Boat Series, San Francisco, 1988
B. Maxis at St. Tropez
C. Bill Koch and George Coumantaros with the Matador crew
D. ICAYA owners admiring the fleet

B

C

D

Sponsorship

Among ICAYA's principal concerns these days are professionalism and sponsorship. Sponsorship of events is acceptable to most members, but sponsorship of boats is not allowed. Whitehouse-Vaux summed it up, "Since professionalism [in sailing] came in, you have two distinct types of people: You've got the mast builders, sailmakers, winch makers, who quite properly want to come along and see how their things are behaving, and that's one thing; but then you've got what we call the 'hired guns,' the people who make a living out of sailing other people's boats, and the sad fact is that unless you are prepared to spend all your time sailing your boat, no matter how good you are, you are not going to be as good as a man who is spending 360 days out of 365 sailing a boat. So we got to the stupid situation where if you wanted to have a reasonable chance of winning, the one thing you couldn't do was to allow the owner to take the wheel. Of course this is completely crazy... A lot of our owners are as good as most professionals, some are not...

"ICAYA has passed a rule requiring owners to steer for at least a reasonable part of the race, not necessarily the first leg. It might be highly dangerous to have a brand-new owner at the wheel on the starting line!" Jim Kilroy, ICAYA Vice-president/Western Hemisphere, essentially agrees, "I don't care who's sailing the other boat, as long as I can trust the son of a bitch on the starting line!" Kilroy is unconcerned about professionalism within ICAYA, and feels that the form and amount of any payments to crew members is up to the owner. "If owners want to stand by and watch someone else steer their boat, that is their business," he declared. Although he personally feels that the new rule requiring the "owners to drive is a wonderful thing because they get to know something about what racing is other than just paying the bills — they have fun out of it," he is opposed to sponsorship of yachts, and believes that people should sail because they want to sail. "If the expenses get out of hand, the process will defeat itself," he added.

Alberini feels that while sponsorship of yachts can and should be regulated, "The problem with attempting to control the number of professional crew is that these boats are very sophisticated machines, and there is a need of highly qualified, well-trained crew on board. They are also, I must say, sometimes dangerous machines because of their size. The new rule requiring the owner to steer for at least part of the race is exactly to maintain the owner's direct involvement with running the boat, and not leave the boat to be 100 percent run by professionals. The presence of 'experienced' crew, tacticians etc. will not be avoided in any case. I think of course it is the natural interest of the owners to have good people on board, and there is an extremely natural interest of the professionals to be involved with the championship that represents the cream of yachting activity.

"What the association is confirming is that no one should pay people to have them on board because of their professionalism. There should be an invitation to race together, and of course there is a tradition that the owners pay for the expenses, but there will be no payment and no potential bidding [among the owners] for professional crew. The relationship should be mainly for personal friendship, or other previous experiences [racing together], not who pays more."

ICAYA rules do not allow sponsored boats to compete against Class 'A' maxis. The owners do not want to be in a position of having to compete financially against a large corporate sponsor which might have a serious vested interest in having its boat win, and therefore spend a disproportionate amount of money to guarantee winning. Certain boats and individual sailors are blacklisted from racing with ICAYA boats because of the completely professional and sponsored nature of their sailing activities.

ICAYA

The Crew

by Roger Vaughan

A maxi crew is the largest team in sports. For day racing around buoys, as many as 30 sailors sandwich themselves between 3,900 square feet of sail and the deep blue sea, doing their best to work smoothly together. This aspect of the maxi fascinated the late Herbert von Karajan, music director of the Berlin Philharmonic for 34 years, owner of the Frers/Huisman maxi, *Helisara*.

"In what other sport must you coordinate so many people?" he once said after one particularly satisfying afternoon of jibe-sets and headsail changes. "The orchestra is more or less the same. A hundred people responding to a common will. It is a synchronized process that runs like film. Like the rhythm of flying, or driving. With sailing, it is the coordination of people with me and the boat. When it is right, it feels like the boat moves by itself."

Typically, a maxi has a professional captain and permanent, paid crew of four people. This gang maintains the boat and makes sure it gets delivered on time to the various ports of call (Sardinia; St. Thomas; Newport) on the annual 14-to-21 day racing program. The remainder of the crew arrives in time for a practice day or two before racing begins. They are an elite, international lot. Scratch a maxi sailor and you'll find someone who has accumulated tens of thousands of ocean-racing miles in hot boats, or who has a couple America's Cup campaigns under his belt—and plenty of prime time in 50-footers, J-24s, One Designs, Finns, Lasers, or sailboards. Although several ICAYA owners won't admit it, today's maxi crewmen expect to have all expenses reimbursed, and to be paid a fee for racing as well.

Trimmers and tacticians tend to come from the sailmaking ranks, while the mid-deck coffee grinders have been taken over by heavies: often weight-lifters and former pro-footballers. The foredeck is reserved for lean, agile types whose hands, feet, and wits better be quick. In any case, the successful crewman inevitably showed up in the right place at the right time with the right chops and cracked the team. Once he is in the network and gained experience with the forces of such a huge boat, he's in demand.

Maxi boats need more than enthusiastic crewmen. They require the highest level of sailing skills because on a maxi, even the smallest adjustment made inadvertently, or at the wrong time, could cause a disaster. Things could break, rip, tear; people could get hurt. The loads on rigging and lines are immense. Many jobs on the boat involve three or more men coordinating their efforts like riggers moving heavy machinery. When you are part of this team effort, your life and limbs depend on the worth of the rest of the team. Competency is the very least one wishes of a fellow crewman on a maxi.

Maxi boat programs come and go, and so do crewmen, hopping from boat to boat and country to country as if they were in a round robin at the local yacht club. Going to China, mate? See you there. It's a brotherhood, and it's deep.

In many ways, the maxi crew network is the same as any other. A sailor who gets on a J-24 (for instance) and performs well is noticed

and appreciated. He is invited back, becomes a regular, and if he is really good others try to entice him aboard their boats. The difference with the maxi class is the unusual, intense relationship that develops between some of the world's wealthiest men and a bunch of sailors who, for all their considerable sailing talent, are in the "average Joe" category. The maxi owner and his crew are symbiotic, like a shark and its pilot fish. If he can't attract the best of these freewheeling, migrant sailors, the maxi owner's program will founder. For the sailors, the maxi man is the answer to their wildest dreams.

Both maxi owner and crew provide something indispensable the other hasn't got. Resources, vision, organization on the owner's part; youth, strength, endurance, sailing ability and an overwhelming commitment to racing (availability) on the part of the crewmen. The tie that firmly binds them is their love of the sea, their obsession to race the biggest and grandest boats in the ocean. While important callers may be snared in the maxi man's tangle of secretaries, crewmen are put right through to the boss. And when the owner summons, crewmen grab a bag and hop on the next jet.

Because of the parity established, the owner/crew relationship on board is always interesting. The boat is common ground. Titles and size of fortune account for nothing in mid-ocean. Certainly the owner is in charge. although in most cases his captain runs the boat. But the prudent owner doesn't go in for muscle-flexing because the crew will flex back. Humor is usually the foundation of successful owner/crew communication. One long-time owner was regularly sent below by the crew when the action on deck got hot. It was done with a series of jokes and one-liners. Even the owner got a good laugh out of it, and it succeeded in removing him from the deck where even he acknowledged that he was a liability.

In the development of the maxi class, there are several programs that have been pivotal. Californian Jim Kilroy, who has owned a succession of five maxis named *Kialoa*, probably formulated the seminal maxi program. There were several big boats that raced at the high end of the Cruising Club of America (CCA) ratings in the 1950s and 60s, but until this compulsive organization man entered the fray, the approach to the big boat was comparatively casual. Hooked on sailing from the time he won a day on the water as a newspaper delivery boy, Kilroy's boats grew at the same rate as his industrial real estate business. In 1964 he moved from a 50-foot yawl to a 73-footer, rated a maxi under CCA. Even in those days the initial investment ($500,000), followed by sails ($70,000) hull modifications, maintenance, and the cost of campaigning ($250,000 annually), took the project out of the realm of "casual sport" or "hobby." It was a business, albeit a sporting one, and Kilroy approached it as such. Kilroy applied the same principals that had worked for him in real estate: "Controlled Averages," and the "Directed Collective."

"I give people an objective and outline the game plan," Kilroy says in rapid-fire jargon: "But I want their execution of it to be operable

within their personal styles in order to get the performance we want. There are many different approaches, and I learn from all of them. So in the end what we have is a directed 'collective' of people bracketed within a stated objective, offering plenty of input, and, of course, abiding by a unilateral decision in the end."

In addition to the full-time captain and crew, Kilroy employed a shore boss to handle logistics for the boat. The shore boss had a list of 50 sailors with whom he communicated regularly. Each was presented with the racing schedule for the year and asked to indicate which races he could make. Each crewman was expected to under-write his own plane ticket, after which Kilroy would provide food and lodging. It was Kilroy's way of encouraging independence. "I don't want zombies around me...I want people who think."

Kilroy didn't want to harbor boat bums. He wanted his crewmen to be working hard to develop their careers. Sailors arriving to race on *Kialoa* could expect a thorough grilling — fatherly but firm — about how they were doing in business, usually followed by a word or two of advice. If, after two years, Kilroy didn't see advancement in a crewman's career, he would be removed from the *Kialoa* list. Several regular *Kialoa* sailors ended up working for Kilroy Industries.

The rest of the rules were simple: no women allowed to sleep on board; put the toilet lid down so towels won't fall in; keep clean sheets on your bunk and make it when not in it; keep your gear and yourself clean; speak your piece then follow orders. The Directed Collective.

It worked. That no more than fifty names were on the list reflected the positive and sustained response to Kilroy's program. One classic sailors' fantasy involves a dream boat of majestic proportions that plies the oceans of the world making a hundred mysterious landfalls, each more enchanting than the last, with its crew sampling the world's cultures, foods, wines and women. Kilroy made it a reality, and a palatable one. Not only that, *Kialoa* took the lion's share of the silver. Until the 80s, when competition in the maxi class escalated, *Kialoa* was always the boat (the organization) to beat.

No maxi ever built can match *Windward Passage I* for pure glamour. Just the drop of her name at a sailor's bar can focus attention and start a long conversation.

Passage was built on the beach in Freeport, Bahamas, by many of the men who would race her. The late Robert Johnson, a freewheeling lumber magnate from Portland, Oregon, chartered the beloved Herreshoff ketch *Ticonderoga* for the Honolulu Race. He was so taken with *Ti* that he bought her by radio telephone half way to Hawaii. After the race he refit the boat and began a three-year racing campaign during which he met British designer Alan Gurney and commissioned him to design *Windward Passage I* .

Zia's former captain, Irmin Stawiki, who had sailed 90,000 miles with Johnson, and who had left yachting to start a construction business in Freeport, poured a cement slab on which to build the boat on the Freeport waterfront. Johnson hired a builder named Carl Chapman from California to supervise construction of *Passage*, and began assembling guys who had sailed with him to work with Chapman on the boat. The legend began.

Johnson owned a restaurant in Freeport, so there were plenty of paying jobs for the "builders," who were working on the boat for the joy of it (ah, the 60s). According to those who were there, there hadn't been so much fun during a project since the Marx Brothers retired.

After *Passage* was launched in 1967, she began a 10-year racing campaign all over the world. A nucleus of the crew who built the boat stayed in the program the whole time, even after owner Johnson died in 1969. "He was a wonderful guy," Irmain Stawiki says of Johnson. "A character, a bit difficult because of that, but super to sail with. He was best man at my wedding. He used to write regular letters to crewmen who couldn't make a race about how we did and what happened. He signed them, 'Capt. Tuna, Chicken of the Sea.'"

The boat Alan Gurney drew was extraordinary, a breakthrough for its time. A few years ago *Passage* came back on the circuit for one season. With her old age allowance, she more than held her own. "If someone wanted to gut her and give her a big face lift, I'll bet she could still be competive," Stawiki says, getting excited about the idea, "and she's more than 20 years old."

Passage crewmen were a loyal bunch who were welcomed aboard other maxis after their program came to a halt. Having credentials from *Windward Passage I* was carte blanche in the international sailing fraternity.

In the early 1980s, Marvin Green, a New York television executive, envisioned a maxi boat. His prerequisites were challenging. "Green said, 'Build me the fastest, prettiest boat in the world,'" his former skipper Mike Keyworth recalls. "His plan at the outset was to campaign the boat on the racing circuit for two years, then convert it for cruising and go sailing with his family. He wanted comfort as well as speed."

Designer David Pedrick drew *Nirvana*, and it filled the bill. In fact, with its teak decks and handsome interior, it raised a lot of eyebrows among the serious, weight-conscious racing crowd. "We did luxury deliveries with the boat," Keyworth says. "On one trip across the Pacific, we had clean sheets every day."

Nirvana raised eyebrows even higher when she won the Newport/Bermuda Race a month after she was launched, setting a course record she still owns.

"Above all else, Marvin wanted to sail with his friends," David Pedrick says. "If it wasn't going to be fun, Marvin's attitude was 'why bother?' *Nirvana* represented the effort of an amateur yachtsman with an amateur crew. The closest guy we had to a hired gun was Steve Colgate, and as it happened, Steve was a friend of Marvin's."

The *Nirvana* program was a grand scheme that ranged from China to Cuba. Only last minute state business kept Fidel Castro from sailing on the boat. "We had a heavy social agenda," Mike Keyworth says. "It was a program that couldn't be duplicated today. First of all, the maxis — other than the Whitbread boats — don't go anywhere. They race around the buoys. And they are all stripped-out day racers now. Marvin used to take pride in occasionally beating *Kialoa*, then inviting Jim Kilroy over for a cocktail in luxurious comfort...right after the race. Of course Jim was our example of how to put a maxi program together. We just tried to go a few steps further.

"My wife sailed with us, and on board we had a real nuclear family. People from *Nirvana*'s racing days are sailing on a variety of the new maxis, or skippering big boats, and they are scattered throughout the marine industry. I have a warm spot in my heart for all those guys."

It's rare when a newcomer has the impact on a sport that Bill Koch has had on the maxi class. In 1983, a change in his career and financial fortunes suddenly gave Koch (pronounced "Coke") the latitude to do virtually anything he wanted. Sailing had tantalized him for years — he has a notable sea captain as an ancestor — so he plunged in with gusto. He first raced in the 1983 SORC on a 55-footer, and learned what "small" was. "It took forever to do the St. Petersberg/Fort Lauderdale Race," Koch Said. "The maxis left us in the dust, and they looked like fun. I decided I liked big boats." For Koch, who is 6'5, it was a logical decision.

Koch's first boat was a Little Harbor 85. Ted Hood skippered, while Koch learned the ropes. They didn't do well. "But I liked racing," Koch said. "Cruising—there is no objective. You eat and drink too much, and there's nothing for the crew to do." Hood began talking to Koch about a breakthrough 90-footer that would rate 70 under the IOR. Then a friend introduced Koch to Jerry Milgram, the sailing wizard at MIT, where Koch had earned two PhD degrees (Chemistry and hydrodynamics). Koch, the new boy with a fresh, scientific eye, posed the eternal question: how do you figure out in advance how fast a boat is going to be?

While Milgram began further work on the familiar problem, Koch bought *Huaso*, a three year-old maxi. He gutted the boat, painted it black, and changed the name to *Matador*, after a family cattle ranch in Texas. He paid the Picasso estate $500 for permission to use two bull heads from paintings as *Matador*'s logotypes, and went racing.

"We did poorly at first," Koch says. "In analyzing why, it came down to the crew. My skipper had loaded the boat with rock stars. We had a crew of egomaniacs."

Koch took over crew selection. "I evaluated each applicant on attitude, ability as a team player, and sailing ability — in that order. I gave ten points for each category, with 30 being a perfect score. It took a minimum score of 9.5 on attitude and teamwork; an average of 6 on sailing ability. We started doing much better, 2nds and 3rds. We got a 2nd in the worlds with a broken mast."

Koch put effort into crew motivation. He bought uniforms and insisted they be worn, and worn properly with the shirts tucked in. "We are a team, we should look like one." He divided the boat into team sectors: bow, mast, grinders, trimmers, afterguard. "The crew boss gave everyone a job so he would feel like part of the family. We developed *Matador* spirit."

Koch awarded a prize after each series of races to the crewman who best exemplified the right attitude and degree of teamwork. "I used to pick the winner, then I began asking the winners to pick. I sailed on other boats and saw anger and hostility. On *Matador* it has been harmonious, pleasant, fun, like a brotherhood."

Meanwhile, Koch has spent in excess of a reported $1 million in his quest to discover why boats go fast, and how to predict performance. Under Milgram's surveillance, Koch funded a program at MIT in basic go-fast research, another to evaluate more than 40 designs that were submitted for his new maxi. He built 25 quarter-scale models of the best designs for tank testing, then put sailing rigs on the 15 hulls that tested fastest and raced them against one other.

A design by Bill Cook was finally selected. The new *Matador*, an 84-footer, was built of composites by Eric Goetz, and launched in May of 1990. While the maxi world waited anxiously to see the result of this exhaustive, scientific approach, one thing was certain: Koch's crew had the right attitude, their shirts were tucked in, and they were ready to give the new boat their best shot.

Boomerang

Registry: USA
Owner/skipper: George S. Coumantaros
Sail no. US 37000
Captain: Jeffrey Neuberth
Designer: German Frers
Builder: Robert E. Derecktor
Year: 1984
IOR-rating: 70.0'
LOA: 24.56m/ 80.5'
LWL: 20.20m/ 66.3'
Beam: 6.00m/ 19.7'
Draft: 3.85m/ 12.6'
Displ: 35.000kg/ 80,279lbs.
Sail loft: North
Mainsail: 156.39m/ 1,683sq.ft.
Headsail: 215.94m/ 2,324sq.ft.
Spinnaker: 478.01m/ 5.145sq.ft.
Winches: Barient
Mast/rig type: Hall Spars/masthead
Construction material: Aluminum 5083
Construction methods: Welded
Engine: Volvo 265 HP
Electronics: Furuno radar
  Furuno Satnav
  Trimble Loran
  Northstar Loran
  Skanti HF
  Robertson VHF
  Ockam
  IBM PC

Boomerang

Owner: George S. Coumantaros
Personal: 67-years-old. Lives in New York with wife Sophie. Has four children and four grandchildren.
Professional Background: Shipping
Sailing Background: Started racing in 1954, although owned a cruising yacht as early as 1948. Has owned four racing boats and two cruising boats.
 "I am interested in sailing because it is one of the sports that really brings you close to nature and forces you to muster all your talents in order to use the wind and the sea to your advantage."
Nautical Miles Logged: Over 20,000
Best Sailing Experience: Racing in the San Francisco and Sardinia Maxi Regattas.
Worst Experience: The 1979 Fastnet.
About *Boomerang*: "I requested the designer, German Frers, to build a maxi boat that would be a breakthrough from the standard maxi boats, be competitive and also comfortable to race in."
 Boomerang has been an outstanding yacht and has won almost every race she entered up to 1988, such as the Honolulu Clipper Race, St. Francis Big Boat Series, The World Maxi Championship of 1985 and many other local U.S. races. Said Coumantaros, "The one prize that has eluded us is the Bermuda Trophy which we are going to try to win in 1990."
About Crew: Crews on *Boomerang* have been outstanding. Most of them have raced on *Boomerang* for quite a few years. "Having raced for so long, we have seen quite a few number of our crew who joined us as college kids get married and have children (who my wife Sophie and I consider as our own grandchildren) and then get bogged down with their businesses and in some instances quit sailing."
Future: Improve *Boomerang* as much as possible and start designing a maxi that will be a new breakthrough. The new boat will be ready for the 1991 racing season.

Boomerang, with her midnight-blue hull and deep-red spinnaker, is perhaps the most stunning maxi on the circuit. Owner George Coumantaros and his crew enjoy a long history of sailing together. In August, 1989, Boomerang *lost her mast at the Sardinia races two-and-one-half months after a major refit in Newport, Rhode Island.....one of the hazards of the sport.*

Boomerang

Congere VI

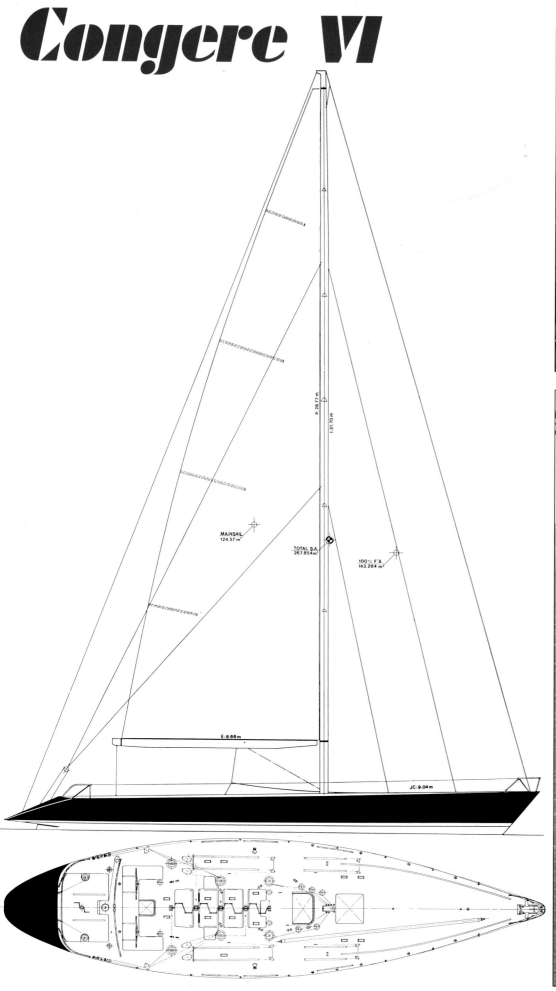

MAINSAIL
124.57 m²

TOTAL S.A.
267.854 m²

100 % F'A
143.284 m²

P: 28.77 m

I: 31.70 m

E: 8.66 m

JC: 9.04 m

Registry: USA
Owner/skipper: Bevin D.Koeppel
Sail no. US 6
Designer: German Frers
Builder: Merrifield-Roberts, Inc.
Year: 1987
IOR-rating: 69.93'
LOA: 23.49m/ 77.07'
LWL: 19.20m/ 63.0'
Beam: 5.88m/ 19.3'
Draft: 3.98m/ 19.3'
Displ: 40,000kg/ 88,183lbs.
Ballast: 19,640kg/ 43,298lbs.
Sail loft: North, San Diego
Mainsail: 144.09m/ 1,551sq.ft.
Headsail: 221.62m/ 2,386sq.ft.
Spinnaker: 480.51m/ 5,172sq.ft.
Winches: Barient
Mast/rig type: Masthead
Construction material: Aluminum
Construction method: Welded
Engine: Volvo TAMD 61A

Bevin Koeppel has raced extensively — the Olympic course, inshore races, and offshore. On February 5, 1990, during the Buenos Aires-to-Rio Race, Congere ran aground 250 miles south of Rio Grande, Brazil, 400 miles into the 1,200-mile race. When she hit the sandbar, the mast broke at the checkstays but the crew was able to secure the mast and prevent it from puncturing the hull.

Fortunately, the boat was only 100 yards from shore. One crew member swam ashore with a line and the others were pulled in. None of the 25 crew members were seriously injured. The boat, after six hours of pounding in the surf, lost her keel and eventually washed up on shore. Her sand-filled hull now lies derelict on an isolated spit of land off the coast of Brazil.

Editor's note: Bevin Koeppel did not wish to be interviewed for this book.

Congere VI

Drumbeat

Owner: Alan Bond

Personal: 53-years-old. Nickname "Bondy." Married Eileen ("Red") Hughes at age 19. Four children.

Profession: Entrepreneur

Professional Background: Migrated to western Australia with English parents at age 13. Left school at age 14 to become sign writing apprentice. Within decade of starting business, Nu-Signs, he was a multi-millionaire. Named Australian of the Year in 1977.

Sailing Background: First sailed in a Cadet dinghy on Perth's Swan River. Started racing in 1967 with purchase of *Panamuna*. Hooked on the sport, commissioned the late Ben Lexcen to design a fast ocean racer, *Apollo*, which won many big bluewater classics.

In 1974 decided to challenge for the America's Cup, the first of five Cup campaigns.

Best Sailing Experience: September, 1983, when Bond broke the New York Yacht Club's 132-year tenure on the America's Cup with the Lexcen designed winged-keel 12-meter *Australia II*.

Worst Experience: His first Newport-Bermuda race when *Apollo* hit a storm with winds of up to 60 knots. The crew nursed *Apollo* into Bermuda under a storm jib.

About *Drumbeat*: Spent $3 million to build state-of-the-art maxi. Designed by David Pedrick, with considerable input by project manager and design co-ordinator Skip Lissiman.

The space-age supermaxi was built from space-age materials — laminates of carbon fiber with a core of nomex. Below decks *Drumbeat* is spartan, but the design allows for a module to be fitted in order to give the owner a small stateroom.

In the 1989 maxi championships, with world champion Peter Gilmour at the helm, *Drumbeat* proved herself to be an extremely fast, but fragile, racing machine. She defeated ultimate winner *Longobarda* in two races at Palma de Mallorca.

Future: "Our plans are indefinite at this stage."

DANIEL FORSTER

Registry: Australia
Owner/skipper: Alan Bond
Sail no. KA R2
Captain: Peter Gilmour
Designer: David Pedrick
Builder: Peter Milner
Year: 1989
IOR-rating: 70.04'
LOA: 25.06m/ 82.22'
LWL: 20.40m/ 66.93'
Beam: 6.13m/ 20.11'
Draft: 4.34m/ 14.24'
Displ: 37,200kg/ 91,274lbs.
Sail loft: North, Sydney
Mainsail: 269.82m/ 2,904sq.ft.
Headsail: 180.59m/ 1,944sq.ft.
Spinnaker: 399.76m/ 4,303sq.ft.
Winches: Lewmar
Mast/rig type: Fractional
Constr. material: Composite
Constr. method: Vacuum Bagged
Engine: Perkins
Electronics: Ockam
   Extensive on board computer

Drumbeat

Drumbeat, *a newcomer to the maxi circuit in 1989, though with an extremely experienced crew, was a hot bet for the Championship. Unfortunately, because Alan Bond was distracted with business difficulties Drumbeat did not get a chance to race in the final regatta at St. Tropez. She was, however, shipped back to Australia in time to compete in the Sydney-Hobart Race, which she won.*

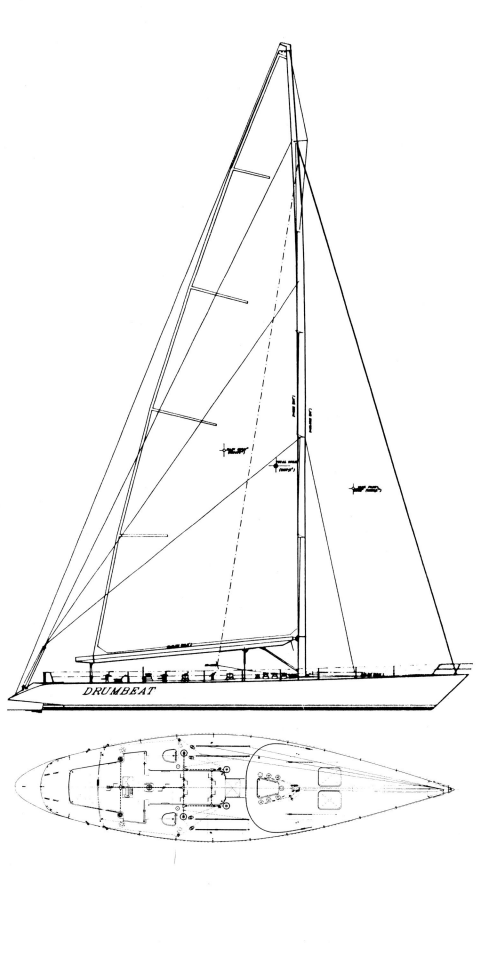

Drumbeat

Emeraude

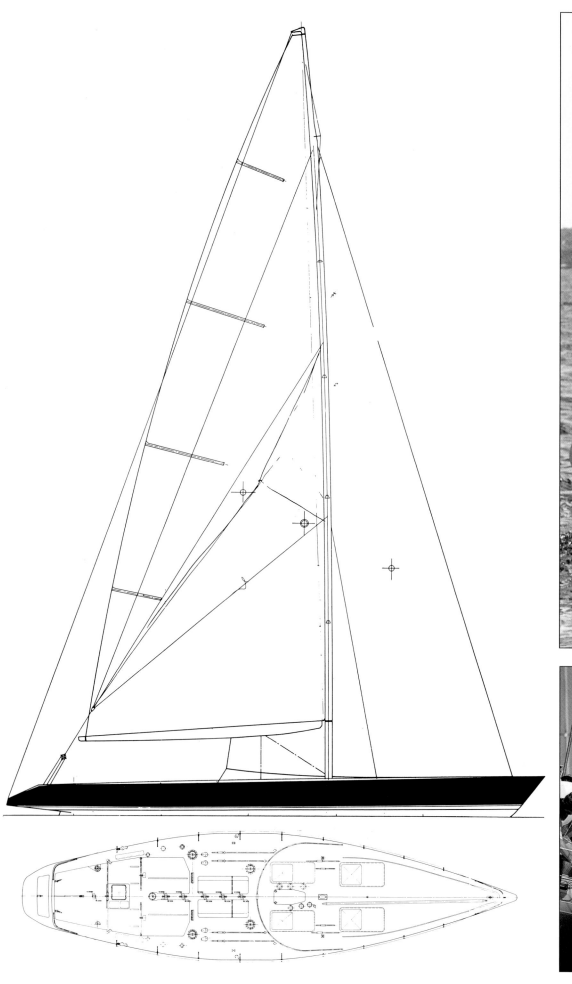

Registry: France
Owner/skipper: Jacques Dewailly
Sail no. F9333
Captain: Mick Harvey
Designer: German Frers
Builder: Eric Goetz
Year: 1989
IOR-rating: 70.05'
LOA: 24.25m/ 79.6'
LWL: 19.70m/ 64.6'
Beam: 6.10m/ 20.0'
Draft: 4.20m/ 13.8'
Displ: 35,600kg/ 77,160lbs.
Ballast: 22,750kg/ 50,154lbs.
Sail loft: North, San Diego
Mainsail: 190.85m/ 2,054sq.ft.
Headsail: 173.69m/ 1,870sq.ft.
Spinnaker: 384.47m/ 4,139sq.ft.
Winches: Barient
Mast/rig type: Sparcraft/fractional
Constr. material: Composite
Constr. method: Vacuum Bagged
Engine: Caterpillar 3208
Electronics:
  Zenith Data Systems
   - SuperSport
  Diconix 150 printer
  Magnavox MX4102 Satellite
   Navigator
  ICOM IC-M55 VHF
  ICOM IC-M11 handheld VHF
  Trimble Navigation
   - Loran-GPS 10X
  Ockam Instruments, Milford, CT
  Rigel Digital Barograph

Emeraude

A mere two weeks after her sea trials, Emeraude raced the 1989 Newport competition where she finished second (but with the same score as the winner). Four days before the regatta started, during a sail trim, she cracked a running backstay fitting, which was repaired the same day, enabling the crew to carry on with their training.

Owner: Jacques Dewailly

Personal: 68-years-old. Married, one son.

Professional Background: Studied engineering. President of a company that provides complete maintenance and support services to large business and residential buildings. Based in France, but extends to other European countries. Recently started a small company in the United States.

Sailing Background: Started with small power boats in l967. Was taken sailing by a friend in l968 and was hooked. ("From that day my interest was only sailing boats...") Has had a succession of five yachts, all called *Emeraude*. Placed fifth in the Fastnet with first *Emeraude*.

Nautical Miles Logged: Estimates 1,000 miles a year for last 20 years.

Best Sailing Experience: Winning the SORC in 1986 when *Emeraude* had just been launched.

Worst Experience: A night race with a Mistral blowing up to Force 11, near Marseille. Many were seasick and all were frightened. It was a terrible experience even though they won.

About *Emeraude*: "When I went to German Frers for my new *Emeraude*, I asked him to design a yacht without extremes, but good in 15-35 knots of wind." It was decided to sacrifice light air performance and concentrate on the conditions prevailing at most ICAYA races.

Emeraude raced in Newport only three weeks after she was launched and tied for first place, although she officially classified as second, based on her overall standings.

About Crew: Almost entirely a carry-over from the previous *Emeraude* — mainly from the U.S., but also from France and Italy. Except for the four permanent hands hired to maintain the yacht the crew is strictly amateur. All have other professions and race just for the fun of it.

Future: Continue racing with the current *Emeraude*, and follow the ICAYA fleet.

Emeraude

Hispania

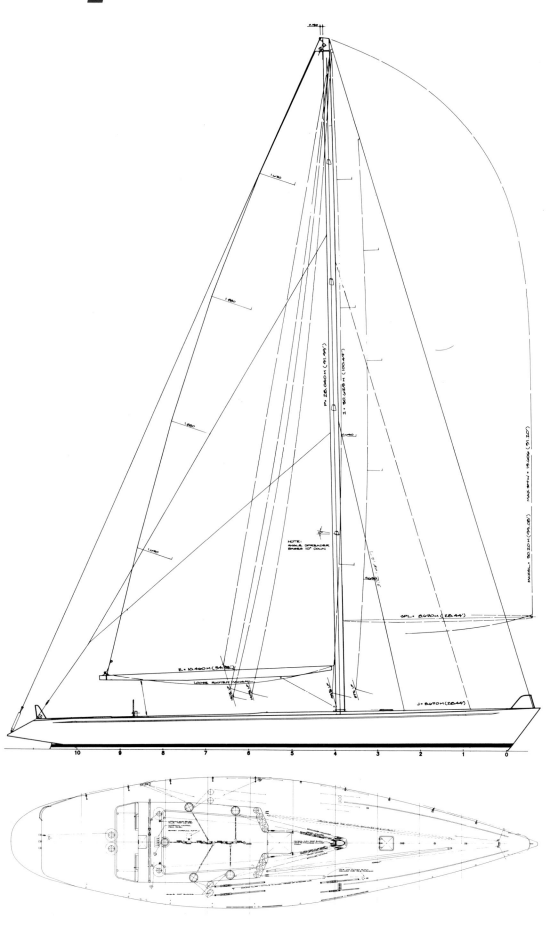

Skipper: Juan Carlos Rodriguez-Toubes

Personal: 45-years-old. Born into a Spanish Navy family (grandfather, father and three brothers are in Navy).

Profession: Commander in Spanish Navy. Also manages Spain's America's Cup challenge — including design, construction, training and overall preparation.

Sailing Background: Started sailing as a child, first in Snipes, then Flying Dutchmen and Stars. In 1968 started racing 3/4 tonners and one-tonners for the Navy. Sailed for six years aboard the training ship *Americana*; during that period did a circumnavigation.

Nautical Miles Logged: No idea.

Most Memorable Sailing Experience: "We were in first position in the Marstrand long-distance race. We were leading just in front of three or four boats when the wind freshened a lot. The others took down their spinnaker while we kept ours up for another 10 minutes. We built up some ground between the others and us, and I really believed we would win the World Championship, but five hours later we broke the mast. Since it was night and we did not have an engine, we had to use flares."

About *Hispania*: Juan Carlos had worked before with Bruce Farr. "We always have had [lengthy] discussions since we want our Spanish ideas included in the designs. Before *Hispania*, maxi yachts were half-cruisers and half-racers. The first design from Bruce followed that trend and I told him I wanted a racer just like a one-ton boat. We started to throw everything away, on deck as well as below. We would have on board only the most essential gear for racing. We had some arguments with Bruce, but finally we got *Hispania*. She was the first thoroughbred inshore maxi. Now all the new maxis are like *Hispania*." The keel was lightened by one ton. Her new keel is designed for downwind sailing, and she lost some stability, but the larger crew (20 crew) helped compensate for that loss.

"When we trained against *Il Moro di Venezia III*, we found our strong and weak areas. We had a new Fin keel fitted, instead of the bulb keel. I believe that we now are the fastest maxi downwind in light air."

About Crew: There are five Navy officers on board, a chief petty officer, 18 enlisted men and a civilian. For several years the Danish sailmaker, Ib Ussing Andersen, sailed with the team. "Now we must learn to do the sailing ourselves but we use Ib as our coach and sailmaker."

Future: *Hispania* will be used as a training boat to test out ideas.

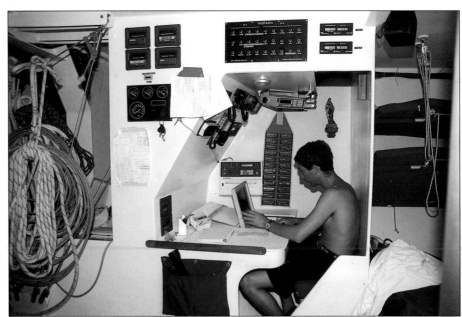

Hispania

Registry: Spain
Owner: Spanish Navy
Sail no. E-10000
Skipper: Juan Carlos Rodriguez-Toubes
Designer: Bruce Farr
Builder: Astilleros Barracuda
Year: 1987
IOR-rating: 70'
LOA: 24.48m/ 80.3'
LWL: 19.68m/ 64.6'
Beam: 6.07m/ 19.9'
Draft: 4.33m/ 14.2'
Displ: 38,198kg/ 84,211lbs.
Sail loft: Diamond - North
Mainsail: 169.00m/ 1,819sq.ft.
Headsail: 207.00m/ 2,228sq.ft.
Spinnaker: 382.00m/ 4,112sq.ft.
Winches: Barient
Mast/rig type: Sparcraft/Masthead
Construction material: FRP composite
Construction methods: Vacuum bagged
Engine: Volvo 130 CU
Electronics: ICOM VHF IC-M100
  ICOM HF IC-M700UK
  Digital Weathercheck - Banair
  Navstar 603S Transit Satellite Navigator
  Furuno radar
  Zenith PC 2X
  Ockam
  Trimble Navigation Loran-GPS-10X

Being the largest IOR racer in Spain, it has taken the crew of Hispania time to learn how to handle this unique boat. She was the only stripped-out inshore maxi racer competing in the 1988 Discovery Race. She was able to take advantage of that 3,830 nautical mile race and use it as a training ground. During three subsequent championship regattas the crew did well but the equipment failed. The head foil failed several times, and in St. Tropez, Hispania lost a victory because of it.

Hispania

Il Moro di Venezia III

Registry: Italy
Owner: Raul Gardini
Sail no. I 11111
Captain: Paul Cayard
Designer: German Frers
Builder: S.A.I. Italy
Year: 1987
IOR-rating: 70.05'
LOA: 24.28m/ 79.6'
LWL: 20.0m/ 65.6'
Beam: 6.24m/ 20.5'
Draft: 4.15m/ 13.6'
Displ: 35,600kg/ 78,483lbs.
Sail loft: North
Mainsail: 192.89m/ 2,076sq.ft.
Headsail: 178.86m/ 1,925sq.ft.
Spinnaker: 395.92m/ 4,262sq.ft.
Winches: Barient
Mast/rig type: Sparcraft/fractional
Construction material: Aluminum
Construction methods: Welded
Engine: Fiat AIFO 8061 SM
Electronics: ICOM VHF IC-M100
 Skanti HF-SSB radio TRP 8250S receiver/transmitter
 Magnavox MX 4102 Satellite Navigator
 Northstar 800 Loran C Navigator
 Furuno DFAX
 Zenith Data Systems
 Diconix 150 printer
 B&G Hercules System Depth sounder
 Datamarine Depth sounder
 Ockam
 Trimble Navigation Loran-GPS-10X
 Dytek Water temperature
 Barograph

Editor's Note: *Il Moro di Venezia* was purchased in Spring 1990 by Mr. Gati, who has changed the name to *Vanitas*.

Il Moro di Venezia III

Il Moro di Venezia III

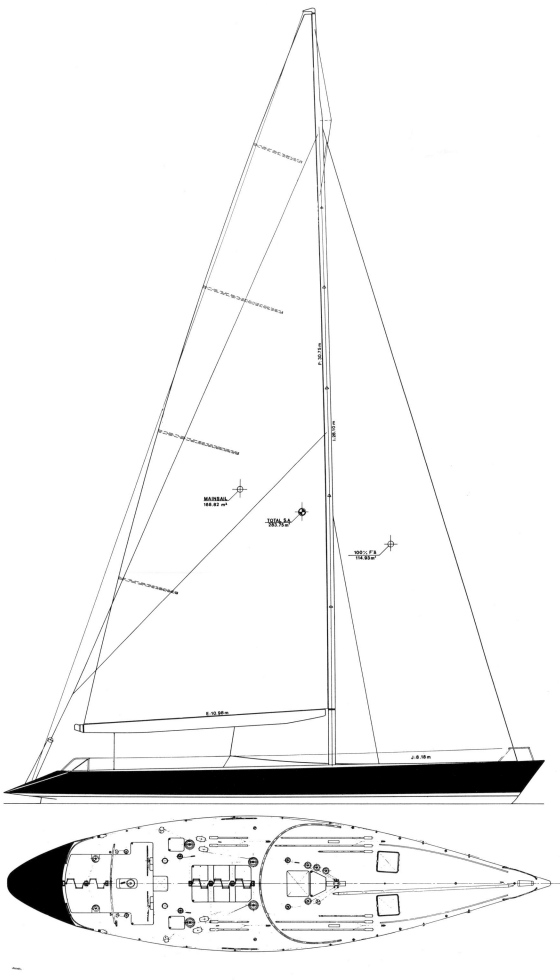

MAINSAIL
168.82 m²

TOTAL S.A.
283.75 m²

100% F'A
114.93 m²

P. 30.75 m

I: 26.10 m

E: 10.98 m

J: 8.18 m

Owner: Raul Gardini

Personal: Born at Ravenna in 1933. Married to Ida Feruzzi; three children.

Professional Background: Studied agronomy at University of Bologna. Began career with Feruzzi Group in 1955. Currently chairman of the board of several major industrial groups.

Sailing Background: Sailed as a child on father's cruising yacht. Was given own sailboat at age 12. Started sailing in international regattas in 1971. Commissioned German Frers to design his first maxi, Il Moro di Venezia, in 1976. She was first to finish the 1979 Fastnet. Launched Il Moro di Venezia II in 1983, and Il Moro di Venezia III in 1987. Both designed by Frers. Il Moro III was Maxi World Champion in 1988, also winning the San Francisco Big Boat series that year. Purchased the ex Windward Passage II, which is now called Passage, to be used to train crew. Il Moro III recently sold.

Best Sailing Experience: Winning the 1988 San Francisco Big Boat Series.

Worst Experience: The 1979 Fastnet.

About Crew: Tries to procure the best talent. For next America's Cup Challenge hired Californian Paul Cayard, a Star Class World Champion, as managing director of the syndicate and potential skipper.

Future: Concentrating on America's Cup Challenge. Gardini approaches racing, particularly America's Cup Challenge, the same way he approaches business. "We will enter the America's Cup to win. I don't see how we could have any other approach!"

Il Moro di Venezia III

Raul Gardini has collected some of the best yachting people from all over the world in sailing, construction and design to be on his team. No other crew would have been able to change the broken mast in St. Tropez in less than 24 hours and be ready for next-day race. The teamwork and high level of competency are obvious aboard Il Moro di Venezia.

Inspiration

Inspiration

Owner: Herbert Dahm

Personal: 60-years-old. Married, with two children, and grandchildren.

Professional Background: Owns and operates several companies in Germany, specializing in marketing consumer electronics, computers and software. Also owns a company that produces aluminum extrusions. "Twenty years ago I gave part of each company to a managing director because I wanted to sail around the world. While searching for a boat, I met Jongert, and since then I have handled the marketing for the Jongert Shipyard...It is more of a hobby than a job."

Sailing Background: Started on the Rhine with a kayak when 10 years old. Later sailed at sea. "When I started my business career I could not sail very much, but once my businesses [were] well under way I got a half tonner." Dahm's boats became larger to accommodate his love of cruising. "I also race where it is fun, and to meet other people.

Nautical Miles Logged: "Perhaps 20-30,000 nautical miles in the 13 boats I have owned."

Best Sailing Experience: "When I was alone on board, sailing from Palma de Mallorca to Porto Cervo. It gives me a great feeling of freedom."

Worst Experience: Delivering a 16-meter boat for a friend. "Close to Cape Finisterre my only crew member, who was seasick, and I encountered a Beaufort 9 storm [that lasted] 36 hours. It was terrible. Luckily the boat was stronger than the crew."

About *Inspiration*: The lines of *Inspiration* were drawn by Ron Holland while the interior was designed by Dahm and Peter Sijm. "When I first saw the American maxi yachts, we had none in Europe. I was inspired to build *Mephisto*, designed by Doug Peterson, a maxi racer with cruising comfort. We sailed against *Kialoa* and *Helisara* with Dennis Conner at the helm. I sold *Mephisto* and built *Inspiration*, but from a new philosophy. I wanted a cruising boat capable of sailing round the world. She became as heavy as a full rating maxi because I wanted a complete, extensive cruising interior and appliances. The speed is not so much less than a thoroughbred maxi racer, which has surprised everybody, and I am pleased with the last four years' racing results. *Inspiration* is a small maxi — rates 60'. Unfortunately, the races are now only for the 70' rated yachts."

Future: "I want to sell *Inspiration* since I want to build a new cruiser/racer — 26 meters or 82 feet, measuring 70 feet IOR — capable of racing on equal terms with the other maxi yachts, but with another philosophy.

"I feel more sailors in the world would like to go cruising with family, friends, live on board, enjoy sailing, and sometimes — not all the time — also go for a good race."

Herbert Dahm

Registry: Germany
Owner: Herbert Dahm
Sail no. G 1913
Captain: Beilken
Designer: Ron Holland
Builder: Jongert, Netherlands
Year: 1985
IOR-rating: 60.18'
LOA: 22.08m/ 72.4'
LWL: 18.30m/ 60.1'
Beam: 5.77m/ 18.9'
Draft: 3.76m/ 12.3'
Displ: 38,000kg/ 83,774lbs.
Sail loft: Beilken, Germany
Mainsail: 126.00m/ 1,356sq.ft.
Headsail: 220.00m/ 2,368sq.ft.
Spinnaker: 450.00m/ 4,844sq.ft.
Winches: Lewmar
Mast/rig type: Rondal/Masthead
Construction material: Aluminum
Construction methods: Welded
Engine: Mercedez Benz OM 407
Generator: Zeise 15Kwa
Waterdesalinator: Mariner Air
Air conditioning: Mariner Air
Electronics: SP Sailor VHF 25 W
  Skanti HF-SSB radio
   TRP 8250S receiver/transmitter
  Furuno DFAX
  Furuno Satellite Navigator
  B&G Hercules 2 system
  B&G Homer 5 Radio
  B&G Compass
  Segatron Autopilot
  Trimble Navigation Loran-GPS-10X
  Koden color radar
  A.P Navigator - decca

Inspiration

Kialoa V

Owner: John B. Kilroy

Personal: 67-years-old, born in Alaska. Married, seven children/stepchildren, all enthusiastic about sports.

Professional Background: Was in the aerodynamics field. As a consequence, finds the technical aspect of sailing fascinating and challenging. Currently builds, owns, rents and/or operates high-rise office buildings. Also owns and manages computer facilities in California, Washington, D.C. and New England.

Sailing Background: Did not sail as a boy, although always involved in water sports. Was a pilot in the Air Force and developed a passion for flying "so you put flying and being around the water together and you have a sailboat!"

Nautical Miles Logged: "I really don't think of it that way. I guess I've probably done as much sailing as anyone."

Best Sailing Experience: "Probably the latest one. You cannot say this was my best, that was my best, because you learn more from your problems and your losses than you do from your victories. Victories you stroke yourself and say 'I did it,' but you may have done it because you were damn lucky. Losses, you probably did it because you were stupid. Well, the greatest thing that happened to me in yachting is that I met my wife through yachting!"

Worst Experience: "Losing through a mental lapse."

About Kialoa V: Kilroy wanted an upwind/downwind boat. Most of the maxi races consist of eight legs: four upwind, two downwind, and two reaches.

"What's happened under the [IOR] rule is a tragedy. When Kialoa V was built she rated 70.04. Today she would rate 68.4, only because of IOR changes to accommodate things that have nothing to do with technical aspects. They felt they were doing us a favor by giving boats rating reductions. Now what they have done is to let huge boats come in, because they have a 70.04 rating, and we in turn have had to do all sorts of things plus spend tremendous amounts of money for rule-oriented changes, not technical changes. I can tell you, I have spent — just for rule-oriented changes, nothing to do with making the boat slower or faster — $400,000 in the last three years. We are going to stabilize the rule within our association so we'll have a fixed rule for five years."

About Crew: "I would say that if you look around this fleet you'd find a tremendous number of ex-Kialoa crew. If you were to take Stars and Stripes in Perth (the 1987 America's Cup), 10 out of the 11 were ex-Kialoa crew.

I do look at taking care of the crew, perhaps in a different way than some people do. I want our crew to look forward not to just the sailing, but to look forward to wherever their future is. And sailing can be a goddess of fun or a goddess of destruction."

Future: This is the last year for Kialoa V. Plans to build a new one when the rules stabilize. Also plans to take a year off from racing and go cruising on Kialoa III, which he has converted to a cruising boat, and do "some of the things that racing has tremendously interfered with!"

"I think the owner is a better owner if he steers, if he knows something about it. He'll command a great deal more respect out of his people."

John B. Kilroy

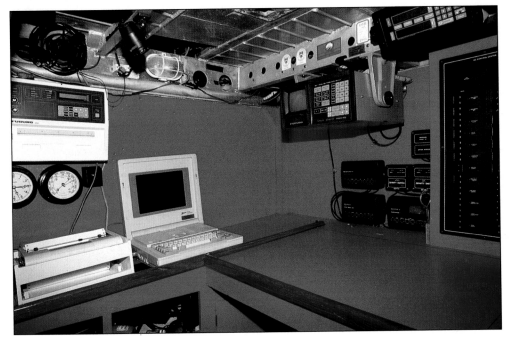

"The crew have to make an effort to sail with us. And I try to help them with their careers. They enjoy it, I enjoy it, we work together, and we've become very dear friends. And they've become a part of what we call the Kialoa family."

"ICAYA sailing — expensive? Let me comment on that, very strongly: people say that it's expensive, but it gives a hell of a lot of people a lot of jobs. They call these maxi yachts. I call them 'marxi yachts' because they redistribute the wealth!"
John B. Kilroy

Kialoa V

F

About ICAYA: "It's the most technical, the most skilled group, the world's best racing. I have been very involved in the principle of fair sailing, because it's no fun if it isn't fair; the last thing that Kialoa wants to do is beat someone by an unfair advantage."

John B. Kilroy

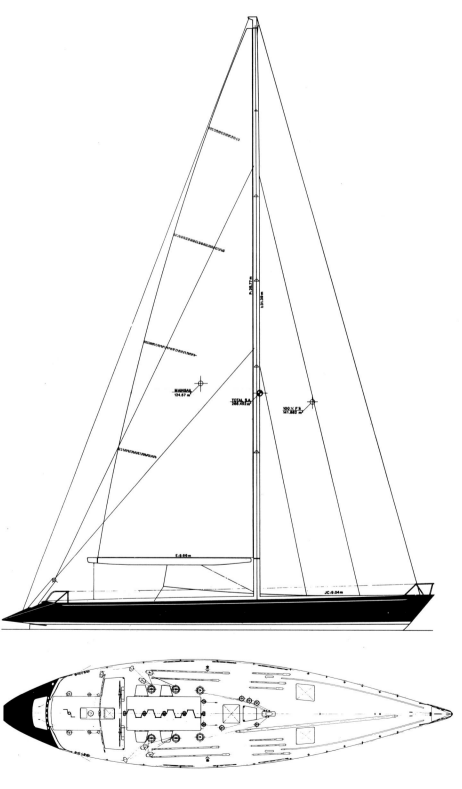

Kialoa V

Registry: USA
Owner: John B. Kilroy
Sail no. US 13131
Designer: German Frers
Builder: Mefasa, Spain
Year: 1986
IOR-rating: 70.05'
LOA: 24.00m/ 78.7'
LWL: 19.60m/ 64.3'
Beam: 5.977m/ 19.6'
Draft: 4.06m/ 13.3'
Displ: 37,820kg/ 83,377lbs.
Ballast: 21,247kg/ 46,841lbs.
Sail loft: North Sails
Mainsail: 148.62m/ 1,600sq.ft.
Headsail: 217.03m/ 2,336sq.ft
Spinnaker: 480.41m/ 5.171sq.ft.
Winches: Lewmar
Mast/rig type: Masthead
Construction material: Aluminum
Construction methods: Welded
Engine: Volvo Penta Tamd 60B
Electronics: Zenith Data System
  Polar Manipulation Program
  Diconix 150 printer
  Furuno DFAX
  Furuno Satellite Navigator
   FSN-70
  Northstar 800 Loran C Navigator
  B&G Hercules System 390
  B&G Hercules System 290
  B&G Hercules System 290
   Depthsounder
  ICOM VHF IC-M56

Kialoa V

"I don't care who's sailing the other boat, as long as I can trust the son of a bitch on the starting line!"
John B. Kilroy

Jim Kilroy has been on the leading edge of inshore racing for more than a decade with a string of competitive Kialoas. His team is the one all the others love to beat. The logo of the world on the transom of Kialoa V is a familiar sight, because so often Kilroy is in the lead!

Kialoa V

Longobarda

Registry: Italy
Owner: Gianni Varasi
Sail no. I-11611
Boat manager: Paolo Cappoli
Captain: Lorenzo Bortolotti
Designer: Bruce Farr
Helmsman: John Bertran
Tactician: John Marshall
Builder: SAI Ambrosini, Italy
Year: 1989
IOR-rating: 70.05'
LOA: 24.32m/ 79.8'
LWL: 19.86m/ 65.2'
Beam: 6.09m/ 20.0'
Draft: 4.31m/ 14.14'
Displ: 37,808kg/ 83,351lbs.
Sail loft: North, Italy
Mainsail: 197.0m/ 2,121sq.ft.
Headsail: 181.0m/ 1,948sq.ft
Spinnaker: 335.0m/ 3,606sq.ft
Winches: Barient
Mast/rig type: Sparcraft/Fractional
Construction material: FRP composite
Construction method: Vacuum Bagging
Engine: Volvo
Electronics: Magnavox MX4102 Satellite Navigator
  Ockam Instruments
  Sailmath computer, software by Graeme Winn
  Diconix 150
  2 x Trimble Navigation - Loran-GPS 10X
    -One on deck and one below deck
  ICOM VHF IC-M80
  Datamarine - International Offshore, Depth Alarm

Longobarda *is a happy boat. On board there is a feeling of confidence and commitment. And why not? Right after being launched, she wasted no time proving herself a winner at Palma de Mallorca! The nationalities of the crew are diverse, but that doesn't seem to present a problem. Laughter and congeniality prevail aboard* Longobarda.

Longobarda

Owner: Gianni Varasi

Personal: 47-years-old. Married, three children.

Professional Background: Owner/major stockholder in glass industry, with offices in Italy, U.S. and South America. Has controlling interest in several European chemical, publishing and real estate companies.

Sailing Background: Started sailing in 1978. Owned several cruising yachts. Sailed extensively in the Pacific, Caribbean, and the Mediterranean. In 1987 bought *Othello* (ex *Il Moro di Venezia II*) from Raul Gardini. Developed a passion for racing. In 1988 decided to remain in the Mediterranean and practice while other maxis went to the Pacific to race. Time was devoted to improving boat handling and developing parameters for a new boat.

Best Sailing Experience: Winning the second race at Palma de Mallorca.

Worst Experience: "When I went from Minorca to Corsica with the rubber boat! ... 240 nautical miles in 15 hours!" (Varasi burst out laughing when he told the story.)

About *Longobarda*: Bruce Farr was requested to design a very light boat that would rate at the top of the maxi class. *Longobarda* was launched July 17, 1989 and won her first race August 2nd of that year. She won all three maxi world championship series at Mallorca, Porto Cervo and St. Tropez.

"When I decided to have a racing boat I wanted to be organized as a business. For everything on board — crew, sails, electronics, etc. — there is a responsible team. And I am very satisfied with the results."

About Crew: There are two project managers: Lorenzo Bortolotti is responsible for the organization of the racing effort, Paolo Cappoli is in charge of the boat. Some of the Americans who have raced with Varasi are John Bertrand, John Marshall and Mike Tober.

Future: "For 1990 we will race in the U.S. and the Caribbean. We do not have any plans to modify the boat, but will concentrate instead on improving her performance."

Longobarda

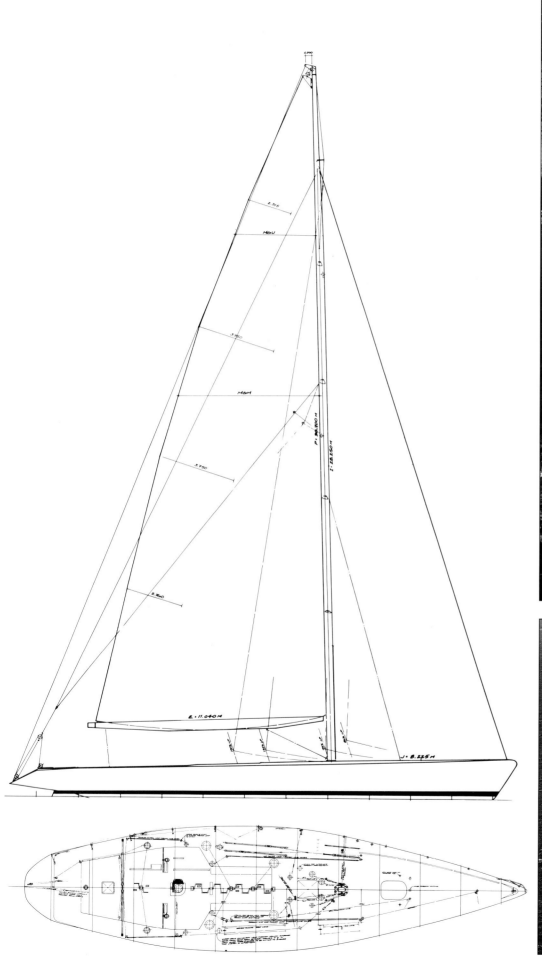

Longobarda

Matador

Matador *is an ultra-clean machine. Bill Koch has ensured that his yacht has state-of-the-art electronics on board. The computers, systems and applications are unsurpassed on the ICAYA circuit. They will no doubt set a precedent for future racing.*

Matador *also employs high tech psychological warfare when it comes to pre-race tactics. When the author of this book was on board taking photos for a 1989 Newport race, he witnessed a highly suggestive pep rally — camaraderie and good spirits prevail aboard* Matador!

Registry: USA
Owner/skipper: William I. Koch
Sail no. US 33955
Captain: Peter Grubb
Designer: German Frers
Builder: Royal Huisman Shipyard
Year: 1983
IOR-rating: 70.01'
LOA: 24.72m/ 81.1'
LWL: 21.40m/ 70.07'
Beam: 6.03m/ 19.8'
Draft: 4.14m/ 13.6'
Displ: 37,500kg/ 82,672lbs.
Sail loft: Sobstad, Halsey, North
Mainsail: 147.69m/ 1,590sq.ft.
Headsail: 206.41m/ 2,222sq.ft.
Spinnaker: 456.91m/ 4.918sq.ft.
Winches: Lewmar
Mast/rig type: Masthead
Construction material: Aluminum 5083
Construction method: Welded
Engine: Mercedes Benz OM 407-6
Electronics: Ockham System - 28 displays
  Anshutz Gyro Compass + 3 displays
  Anshutz Gyro Alarm
  Furuno Radar 72 miles/color with plotter
  Furuno Satellite Navigator FSN-70
  Furuno AD Converter CAD-105
  Sea 223 radio SSB radio telephone
  ICOM SSB IC-M700
  ICOM VHF Transreceiver
  Datamarine Depthsounder
  B&G Hornet 4 Sail Monitor
  2 x Northstar 800 Loran C
  Dytec Seawater temperature display
  Zenith 183 computer with Compusail Software
  2 x Portable 386 computers with custom software

Matador

"My original objectives in getting this boat were to learn about maxi boat racing, to have a good competitive boat, to build the organization, teamwork and crew and all the other kind of stuff, and then to spend two or three years doing testing to try to find out what the fastest maxi boat is. And then build a new boat. So I bought this as kind of a training boat."

William I. Koch

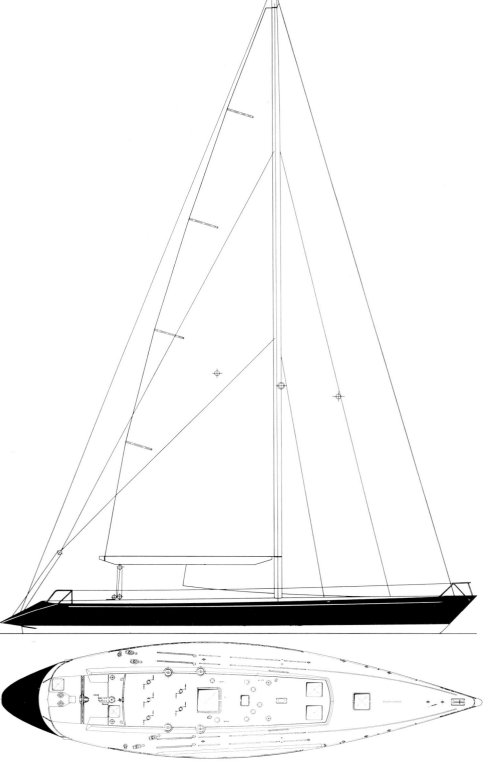

Matador

Owner: William I. Koch

Personal Notes: Born in Kansas, 49-years-old, married, one son. Studied at MIT, where he earned three degrees: Bachelor of Science, Master of Science, Doctor of Science.

Profession: Builds, owns and operates power plants using alternative fuels such as geothermal steam, wood chips, waste products from coal mining. Also in oil and coal, high tech plastics, and real estate.

Sailing Background: Did not grow up in a sailing family. "Well, in Kansas there's virtually no water..." Started sailing at summer school in Indiana at age 12. As a boy — mostly grew up with horses, worked on ranches. "The name *Matador* is from my father's favorite ranch in Texas. While at MIT I occasionally sailed out of Marblehead and I always wanted to own and sail a big boat, so when I got to a position where I could afford to buy one I went out and bought the biggest one I could find. *Matador* is my third boat. I owned a boat with Ted Hood briefly in 1984, also bought an 85' cruising boat that I'm glad I don't own any more..." Bought *Matador* in the fall of 1984.

"I cruised [my cruising boat] in the Bahamas, the Caribbean, and the Galapagos Islands. I got so I didn't enjoy it as much because all I do is eat and drink on board... she wasn't as responsive and as much fun to sail as a maxi boat."

Nautical Miles Logged: About 15,000 nautical miles to date.

Best Sailing Experience: Beating *Boomerang* by half a second (two feet!) in a regatta in Newport. The lead changed about four or five times during the whole race. That was the most exciting.

Worst Experience: Leading *Boomerang* around the course for the world championship while in first place. Going around the last mark *Matador* lost her mast.

About *Matador*: Built in 1982 (as *Huaso*) by the Royal Huisman Shipyard, designed by German Frers. She was designed as a racer/cruiser, with an interior that could be removed for racing. But there were too many compromises, "She was a lousy cruising boat and a lousy racing boat. So I completely gutted the interior, put a new deck on her, did all kinds of things to modify her.

The racing results have been fairly good. Second in world championship three years in a row. In SORC always in top three boats. Won the prize for the most elegant yacht two years in a row in Sardinia.

About Crew: Koch tries to keep the same crew. Has a group of about 60 people who race regularly with him. They are "mostly good friends, good sailors but not professionals. They race as a hobby, for the love of it, for fun."

"I like Jim Kilroy's remark: someone asked him if this isn't a rich man's sport, and he said `no, it isn't: there's one rich man on board and there are 25 poor men and they enjoy it more than the rich man does."

The Future: Planning a new maxi, very high tech. She will be a very unusual boat; construction will begin soon.

Matador

Milene V

Owner: Albert Mirlesse

Personal: Born in Paris; married, six children. 75-years-old. "I am the oldest in the group [of maxi owners] at the moment, but still, I don't feel the strain too much!"

Professional Background: Joined French Navy as a cadet, retired after three years. Joined the Free French Air Force at beginning of World War II. Fought with DeGaulle. After the war became an industrial consultant, assisting developing countries. Worked with the United Nations as technical assistant. Also worked in a consulting capacity with the French government. Became a private consultant in the l960s. "Consulting is strenuous work. Going to sea is for me a relaxation. I started sailing again in 1970, when I had more time as an independent consultant."

Sailing Background: Started in 1932 when he was in the Navy. Didn't sail again until 1970 when he acquired his first boat, a Swan 43, "without knowing much about sailing!" Immediately developed a passion for racing, and sailed the 1971 Fastnet.

Since then has participated in three Admiral's Cups, once with the French team, twice with the Swiss team. Before building *Milene V* he also owned a Swan 48, a Swan 47, and a Swan 441.

Nautical Miles Logged: More than 100,000

Best Sailing Experience: "I have them every day... it's not only winning, but if one performs well, if things go smoothly, then you are happy, and this is the kind of satisfaction one gets."

Worst Experience: The 1979 Fastnet. "...Nothing broken. I was on my Swan 441. Only my airspeed indicator was stuck at 60 knots and wouldn't come down!"

About *Milene V*: The inspiration for building *Milene V* started during a casual meeting with Baron Edmund de Rothschild, who was then outlining the rules and foundation of ICAYA. "The idea of a maxi appealed to me then, although the concept [of ICAYA] today is much different from the original one."

"It certainly is a heavy enterprise! The logistics are heavy. It was a challenge, and I liked the idea of ICAYA, the owners doing it on a personal sport basis without all the commercial aspect usually attached to sailing big boats. I think ICAYA is very protective of this [private] status, of not accepting sponsors."

"*Milene V* was designed by French architect Gilles Vaton. Then I discovered that a maxi boat is never finished, you have to modify for practically every race." It is what Jim Kilroy calls 'changing the configuration.'

About Crew: Mirlesse still maintains the amateur ethic. Crew are mostly working young people with jobs ashore; different from professional crews. "I think it's very important that the crew are all good friends, know each other from weekend racing. The atmosphere on board is very relaxed. We really consider ourselves amateurs, and as such there is always room for improvement. Each time I say well, thank God, the mast has not collapsed, nobody has been hurt today, so it's already an achievement!"

Future: *Milene V* is for sale, and I am thinking about building a large trimaran for fast, record-breaking passages. "I know what it's all about now, it's a lot of work, a lot of management.

"I have very mixed feelings about the future. At an ICAYA meeting, where I was not present, a decision was taken to have no crew limit. Now we have boats sailing with removable ballast, which is exactly the opposite of the IOR rules. I am against it and I find it absurd. Even the new yachts are built in such a way that the crew weight is vital to the hull trim."

Milene V

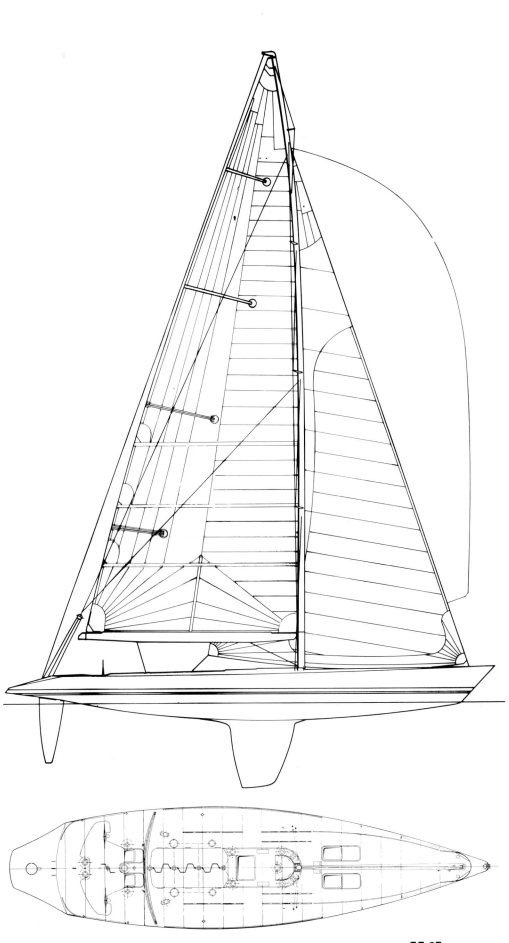

Milene V

Mr. and Mrs. Albert Mirlesse are extremely cordial hosts. The permanent crew — Marie-Claire, Totone, André, Pierre and sailing master Jean — comprise a team with excellent spirit. Milene V was the first boat to allow the author of this book a chance to race in a regatta.

Registry: Jersey
Owner/skipper: Albert Mirlesse
Sail no. K 904
Captain: Jean Guillem
Designer: Gilles Vaton
Builder: Construction Mecanique de Normandie
Year: 1985
IOR-rating: 70.05'
LOA: 24.48m/ 80.3'
LWL: 19.75m/ 64.8'
Beam: 6.20m/ 20.3'
Draft: 4.20m/ 13.8'
Displ: 33,490kg/ 73,832lbs.
Sail loft: North, Germany
Mainsail: 176.20m/ 1,897sq.ft.
Headsail: 163.90m/ 1,764sq.ft.
Spinnaker: 362.70m/ 3,904sq.ft.
Winches: Lewmar
Mast/rig type: Sparcraft/Masthead
Construction material: Epoxy Preimprenated GRP
Construction method: Vacuum Bagged
Engine: Volvo 120 Turbo diesel
Generator: Northern Light
Desalinator: Power Surveiur
Electronics: B&G Hercules System 390
  B&G Hercules 2 System 290 Depthsounder
  B&G Hercules System 390 Computer Unit
  Sailor VHF Type C403
  Trimble Navigation High Accuracy Loran 300
  CRM 1504 PVD19 - phone via VHf in France
  Magnavox MX5102 Satellite Navigator
  Skanti SSB Radio-telephone type TRP8258S

"I think ICAYA is losing some of its spirit. The maxi yachts are confined to an Olympic triangle course, which has made many of the maxis a training ground for the America's Cup."

Albert Mirlesse

"I believe those big boats should not confine themselves to match races or Olympic triangles. Day races and Olympic triangles are misdirected. Maxis should have races like the Fastnet, minimum, [requiring] knowledge of meteorology, navigation.... you live with the ocean, you live with the elements, choose options according to the winds, that is very gratifying."

Albert Mirlesse

Milene V

Mistress Quickly

Owner/Skipper: William Whitehouse-Vaux

Personal: 66-years-old. Married with two grown children. Everyone in family takes an active part in the boat.

Professional Background: ex-Royal Navy, lawyer, diplomat

Sailing Background: Has sailed all his life. (Been racing for 63 years) Takes an active interest in all aspects of racing and organization. Was a founding member of International Class 'A' Yachting Association. Has owned several boats, including six-meter boats, and a 10.5 Meter Cruiser/Racer and currently has two six-meters in addition to *Mistress Quickly*.

Best Sailing Experience: Winning the Middle Sea Race in 1978 by ten hours and setting the course record which still stands today.

Worst Experience: A China Sea typhoon; also 1979 Fastnet Race.

About *Mistress Quickly*: Ex *Ballyhoo*, built in 1974, bought in 1978 and campaigned actively for several years at the following: S.O.R.C., Middle Sea Race, Cowes Weeks, Pan Am Clipper Cup, Antigua Race Weeks. Still holds records for Middle Sea Race and Cowes Round The Island Race. Also holds Trans-Atlantic Record. Won the famous "Birds" Spinnaker in the Fort Lauderdale/Key West Race.

About Crew: Same crewpool since inception — all race the boat with a true Corinthian spirit!

The Future: Who knows?

Remarks: "Flog that man!"

"The crews of today almost certainly are more proficient than the crews of sailing ships in the 'great days of sailing.' Without such crews it would not be possible for a modern maxi to be raced at its upper limits."

William Whitehouse-Vaux

YOICHI YABE

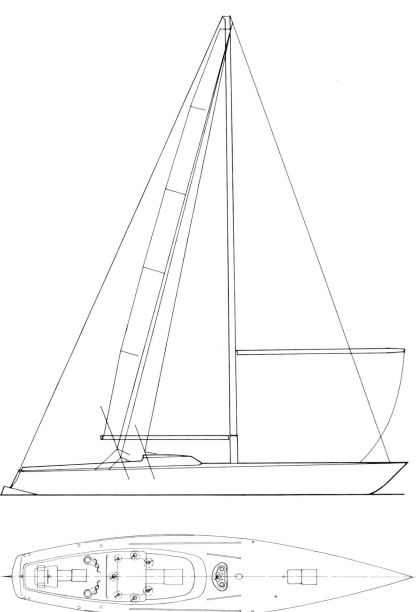

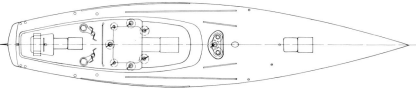

Mistress Quickly

Being the oldest yacht in the fleet with real bunks, a comfortable saloon and a real galley, she still does well at races. She is maintained in bristol condition and every other year has a complete electronic refit. Mistress Quickly has sailed on all seven seas (on her own bottom). When she is not participating in races herself, she often serves as Whitehouse-Vaux's mother ship when he is racing six-meters.

Mistress Quickly

Ondine VII

Registry: England
Owner: Huey Long
Sail no. K 1015
Captain: Joe Jones
Designer: German Frers
Builder: W.A. Souter (Cowes) Ltd.
Year: 1986
IOR-rating: 70.04'
LOA: 24.50m/ 80.38'
LWL: 20.40m/ 67.0'
Beam: 5.98m/ 19.62'
Draft: 4.14m/ 13.58'
Displ: 37,649kg/ 83,000lbs.
Ballast: 20,094kg/ 44,300lbs.
Sail loft: Halsey, Doyle, Sobstad
Mainsail: 152.83m/ 1,645sq.ft.
Headsail: 225.24m/ 2,425sq.ft.
Spinnaker: 498.60m/ 5,367sq.ft.
Winches: Barient
Mast/rig type: Sparcraft/Masthead
Construction material: Composite
Construction method: Vacuum Bagged
Engine: Perkins 240 Turbo
Electronics: B&G Hercules System 390
  B&G Hercules 2 System 290 Depthsounder
  Trimble Loran 300
  Northstar 800 Loran
  Magnavox MX4102 Satellite Navigator
  Datamarine International Offshore Depth Sounder
  Furuno radar 138
  Alden Marine Fax VI
  Sailor VHF type C403
  Hewllet Packard 100 + computer
  Hewllet Packard 9114B Disk Drive
  Hewllet Packard Think Jet Printer
  Skanti SSB Radiotelephone type TRP8250S

Owner: "Huey" Long

Personal: 69-years-old. Born in Boston. Graduated from U.S. Merchant Marine Academy and MIT. Married, three sons.

Profession: Currently in shipping.

Sailing Background: Some sailing on Charles River when young, though not born into a sailing family. Growing up in Boston and being in the shipping business made sailing a natural interest to pursue. Started racing in 1952, and has since sailed many transatlantic races. Participated in almost all major ocean-racing events.

Nautical Miles Logged: At least 200,000

Best Sailing Experience: *Weatherly* beating *Australia* for the America's Cup in 1962. "...And the Australians came to me and said, 'you have the fastest ocean racer in the world, we challenge you to do the toughest ocean race in the world — the Sidney-Hobart— do you accept?' I said yes, and they asked when I would be out there, and I said November 26th, 1400 hours at Sidney Heads. (I'd made an evaluation of the distance). And they all laughed! I showed up at Sidney Heads November 26th at 1406. They had 350 boats meet us. Miss Australia greeted me as I came off the boat... the most dramatic experience of my life! General McArthur could not have gotten a bigger reception!" (Long won the race by 60 seconds, beating a 70' boat with his 57' *Ondine*.)

Worst Experience: "The worst yachting experience always means you lose the mast, or you do something so that you can't finish the race. That happened to us once during the SORC. Once we lost a race to *Kialoa* in Sardinia by 17 seconds. We were ahead of her and lost our tack fitting."

About *Ondine VII*: "The basic problem [for *Ondine*] is that the new boats, with the fractional rigs, have a great advantage because of their additional mainsail area that they are not paying for under the rule. And the fact that they're so light and that they can tack so much quicker than we can — we drop a knot and a half, they drop at the most 8/10ths of a knot, maybe we drop even 1-3/4 knots — so you really have to go for the corners and that's taking quite a chance.."

About Crew: She sails with many crew members from the Swedish America's Cup team. Several are experienced 12-meter sailors. Robbie Doyle has helped a lot with trim and tactics. Tom Wallen put the core group together.

Future: "We have to build a new yacht to be competitive with the new fractional rigs. You can't just remodel the existing boat." Long has not yet decided on a designer. He also plans to wait to see what rule changes occur in November 1989 before deciding what to do.

Ondine VII

"The sport has changed, become a profession, unfortunately, which is very bad. People have been prone to come into the sport and pay to have the best talent on board, and that's contrary to what I have believed in all my life, which was to make it an amateur sport. "

"Huey" Long

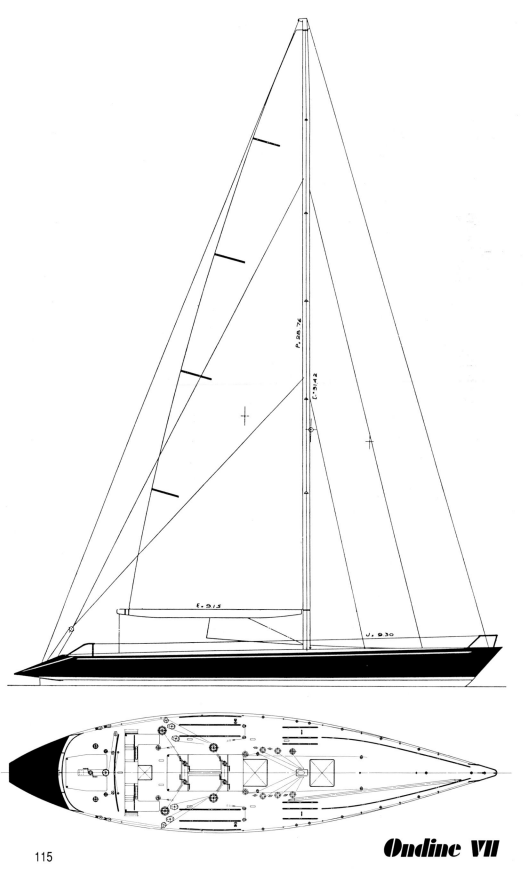

115

Ondine VII

"I used to be a navigator with TWA, so for me it's kind of fun to do the long-distance race. It shows how good your crew and your boat are in all kinds of conditions over a long period of time. But people don't want to do that anymore so the boats are being built unable to withstand the vagaries of the weather that you would encounter in long-distance racing, and they're built on the borderline between safety and speed.

"The Whitbread goes too far as far as I'm concerned. I still have a business to run and I cannot take that much time off. I get a certain enjoyment from racing, but I would not get the same enjoyment spending months at sea. But now we're at the other side of the coin where we're spending [only] several hours racing."

"Huey" Long

Huey Long was the first to invite an America's Cup team (from Sweden) on board for training (later followed by Milene V and Emeraude). The idea was to enable the team to acquire big boat experience. The experience was of mutual benefit, as Ondine VII subsequently did well in the match racing.

Ondine VII

Sovereign

Registry: Australia
Owner/skipper: Bernard Lewis
Sail no. KA 130
Captain: David Kellett
Designer: David Pedrick
Builder: Lewiac Pty. Ltd.
Year: 1986
IOR-rating: 70'
LOA: 25.38m/ 83'3'
LWL: 21.64m/ 71.0'
Beam: 6.09m/ 20'0'
Draft: 4.41m/ 14'6'
Displ: 34,475kg/ 76,000lbs.
Ballast: 19,050kg/ 42,000lbs.
Sail loft: Hood, North
Mainsail: 189.57m/ 2,041sq.ft.
Headsail: 214.86m/ 2,313sq.ft.
Spinnaker: 475.61m/ 5,120sq.ft.
Winches: Lewmar
Mast/rig type: Sparcraft/masthead
Constr. material: Aluminum to ABS standard.
  From 10mm to 4mm plate thickness
Constr. method: Welded
Engine: Perkins Turbo Charge diesel
Generator: Onan 6.5KWA 240 V
Electronics: Satellite Navigation
  Brookes & Gatehouse Hercules 390,
    interface to Apple IIc computer
  Epsom printer
  Radar
  Weatherfax
  UHF and VHF Radio
  Loran

Since she has a red hull and is the biggest of the inshore maxis, *Sovereign is always easy to spot at the races. A crew of hard-core Australians, supplemented with Swedes, Brits and local sailors in Newport proved that good racers only need a few days to get a maxi to top speed.*

Sovereign

Owner: Bernard Lewis

Personal: 55-years-old. Born in Yorkshire, England; grew up in Tasmania, Australia. He and wife Toni have two daughters and a son.

Professional Background: Always worked in real estate and property development, starting with nothing and building his business into a multi-million dollar success.

Sailing Background: Purchased 12-meter *Gretel* (the 1962 Australian Challenger for the America's Cup) in 1972 to promote a development venture. Became "hooked on the beauty, speed, and power of large sailing yachts," and converted her to an ocean racer. Subsequently owned *Vengeance*, which still holds two ocean-racing records won under his ownership.

Best Sailing Experience: "Taking on the world's best in St. Thomas and Newport in 1989 and beating them."

Worst Experience: Retiring from the Sidney-Hobart Race while leading the fleet, due to a sheared bolt in the mast. Also being dismasted during the 1988 San Francisco Big Boat Series.

About *Sovereign*: In November, 1985, gave Dave Pedrick the mandate to design "a maxi yacht capable of being the fastest maxi in the world. She had to be the largest, prettiest yacht afloat on the ICAYA Circuit..." Also requested that she be strongly built and be laid out for both racing and entertaining.

Sovereign won both 1989 ICAYA Series — St. Thomas, USVI, in February and Newport, R.I.— in June, and was the first Australian yacht to win the Sidney-Hobart Race on both line honors and handicap.

About Crew: A nucleus of the same crew members has raced on *Gretel* and on *Vengeance*. The captain and yacht manager for the past 11 years has been David Kellet. "Guest" helmsmen include Peter O'Donnell, Olympic Gold Medalist; Peter Gilmour, *Kookaburra*; and Paul Cayard, Star World Champion.

Future: "It is time to retire *Sovereign* and relax with some cruising... At this stage I do not plan another maxi, but who knows...?"

(Editor's note: Lewis sold boat to Californian Victor Fargo, July, 1989.)

Sovereign

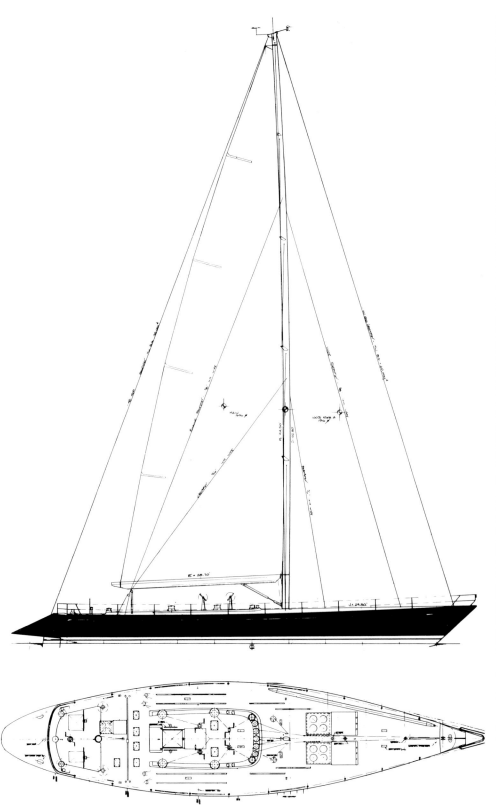

Sovereign

Windward Passage II

Owner: Rod Muir

Personal: Australian. Married, three children.

Professional Background: Owned a group of successful FM radio stations in Australia. Now owns a large farm, where he breeds Arabian horses, makes wine, and is a commercial producer of Watuzi grass. He is also developing a golf course near Sydney.

Sailing Background: "As an Australian I have always liked the sea...my wife Cathy and I share a common devotion for yachting." Started sailing in 1985. Owned a 45-foot sailboat, then a 52-foot power boat. "Soon we felt that to learn even more about sailing, we had to do some racing." Muir bought *Windward Passage I* and started racing. He then built *Windward Passage II.*

About *Windward Passage II*: Muir used state-of-the-art technology, including some techniques that had never been used before in yacht building. Rather than curing the composite hull in an oven, the builder used heating mats to achieve constant temperature throughout. Eschewing the usual aluminum space frame, *WP II* uses carbon prepreg for her structural members. The total weight of her hull and deck is a remarkably light 4,000 lbs.

About Sailing: Two years ago Muir said: "If Cathy and I have to choose between racing and cruising, we shall definitely give up racing. We love the long passages. *Windward Passage I* has been totally refitted, originally as a mother ship to *WP II* and a floating lab for testing *WP II*'s performance. Now it is used as our cruising home. In all, it took 16 months to revamp the boat. But I thought it would be a shame to let that grand lady deteriorate after what she and her previous owners had achieved."

Editors note: *Windward Passage II* was purchased by Italian Raul Gardini in the Fall, 1989 and is now called *Passage.*

NEIL RABINOWITZ

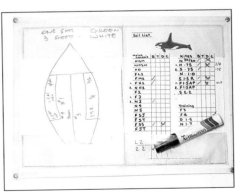

Windward Passage II

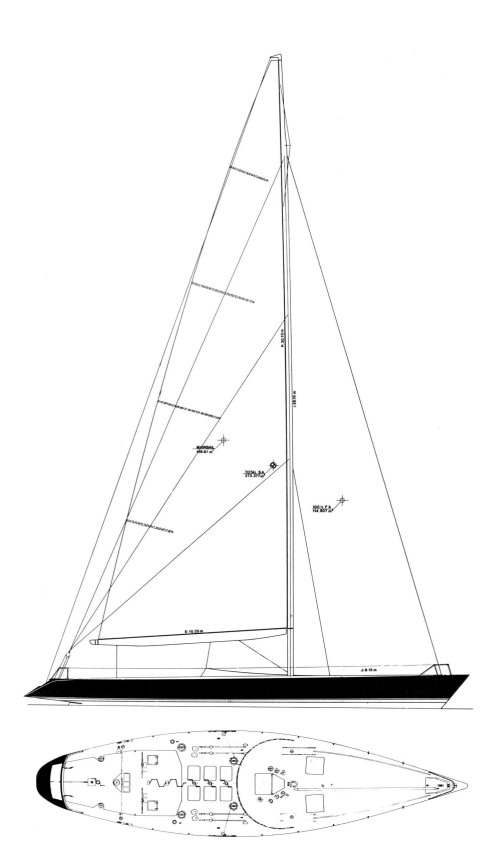

It is easy to spot Windward Passage II with "The Killer Whale" spinnaker flying high. She was the first of the maxis to be built without the use of aluminum frames to take the stress from keel and mast. To lessen pitching, she was also the first not to use any bulkheads forward of the mast and aft of the rudder. Windward Passage II is definitely a state-of-the-art boat.

Registry: Australia
Owner: Rod Muir
Sail no. KA 1988
Captain: John McClure
Designer: German Frers
Builder: McConaghy/SP-Systems
Year: 1988
IOR-rating: 70.05'
LOA: 24.342m/ 79.9'
LWL: 19.7m/ 64.6'
Beam: 6.10m/ 20.0'
Draft: 3.95m/ 13.0'
Displ: 38,100kg/ 83,995lbs.
Ballast: 22,680kg/ 60,000lbs.
Sail loft: Fraser Sails
Mainsail: 178.54m/ 1,922sq.ft.
Headsail: 176.41m/ 1,899sq.ft.
Spinnaker: 390.49m/ 4,203sq.ft.
Winches: Lewmar
Mast/rig type: Whale Spars/fractional
Constr. material: Composite
Constr. method: Bagged
Engine: Detroit Diesel Model 4082-8300

Windward Passage II

*AND OTHER REGATTAS WITH ICAYA PARTICIPATION

1980 SORC
1. Kialoa IV, John B. Kilroy, USA
2. Mistress Quickly, Whitehouse-Vaux, Bermuda
3. Boomerang, George Coumantaros, USA
4. Jader, John Galanis
5. Ondine, Huey Long, England

1980 World Cup — Porto Cervo*
1. Bumblebee IV, Kahlbetzer, Australia
2. Benbow, Giuseppe Recchi, Italy
3. Phantom, Sabasini, Italy
4. Gitana VI, Rothschild, France
5. War Baby, Warren Brown, Bermuda
6. Ikra II, Redele, France

1981 SORC
1. Kialoa IV, John B. Kilroy, USA
2. Bumblebee IV, Kahlbetzer, Australia
3. Champagne Charlie, Alain Gabbay, France
4. Windward Passage I, Johnson, USA
5. Mistress Quickly, Whitehouse-Vaux, Bermuda
6. Xargo IV, Doyle, Spain
7. Gitana VI, Baron de Rothschild, France

Seahorse Race — Cowes
1. Kialoa IV, John B. Kilroy, USA
2. Xargo IV, Doyle, Seitches, Spain
3. Flyer, C. van Rietschoten, Holland
4. Bermuda Condor, Robert Bell, Bermuda
5. Mistress Quickly, Whitehouse-Vaux, Bermuda
6. Ceramco New Zealand, Peter Blake, New Zealand
7. FCF Challenger, Lesly Williams, England
8. Antares, English, France
9. Gitana VI, Baron de Rothschild, France

Porto Cervo
1. Kialoa IV, John B. Kilroy, USA
2. Xargo IV, Seitches/Doyle, Spain
3. Helisara VI, Herbert von Karajan, France
4. Antares, English, France
5. Ondine V, Huey Long, USA
6. Bumblebee IV, Kahlbetzer, Australia
7. Mistress Quickly, Whitehouse-Vaux, Bermuda

1981 World Champion
1. Kialoa IV, John B. Kilroy, USA
2. Bumblebee IV, Kahlbetzer, Australia
3. Xargo IV, Doyle, Spain
4. Mistress Quickly, Whitehouse-Vaux, Bermuda
5. Helisara VI, Herbert von Karajan, France
6. Gitana VI, Rothschild, France

1982 SORC
1. Windward Passage I, USA
2. Kialoa IV, John B. Kilroy, USA
3. Boomerang, George Coumantaros, USA
4. Condor, Robert Bell, Bermuda
5. Ondine V, Huey Long, England

Palma de Mallorca*
1. Nirvana, Marvin H. Green Jr., USA
2. Xargo IV, Doyle, Spain
3. Il Moro di Venezia I, Raul Gardini, Italy
4. Mistress Quickly, Whitehouse-Vaux, Bermuda

Hawaii PanAmClipper Cup*
1. Windward Passage I, Johnson, USA
2. Condor, Robert Bell, Bermuda
3. Kialoa, John B. Kilroy, USA
4. Condor of Bermuda*, Robert Bell, Bermuda
*ex Heath's Condor

Porto Cervo*
1. Helisara, Herbert von Karajan, France
2. Mistress Quickly, Whitehouse-Vaux, Bermuda
3. Nirvana, Marvin Green, USA

1982 St. Francis
1. Kialoa IV, John B. Kilroy, USA
2. Condor of Bermuda, Robert Bell, Bermuda

1983 SORC
1. Kialoa IV, John B. Kilroy, USA
2. Windward Passage I, Johnson, USA
3. Boomerang, George Coumantaros, USA
4. Nirvana, Marvin Green, USA
5. Condor, Robert Bell, Bermuda
6. Midnight Sun, Jan Pehrsson, Sweden
7. Ondine, Huey Long, England

Norway
1. Nirvana, Marvin Green, USA
2. Windward Passage I, Johnson, USA
3. Kialoa IV, John B. Kilroy, USA
4. Ondine V, Huey Long, England
5. Midnight Sun, Jan Pehrsson, Sweden

Palma de Mallorca
1. Kialoa IV, John B. Kilroy, USA
2. Helisara, Herbert von Karajan, France
3. Nirvana, Marvin Green, USA
4. Condor, Robert Bell, Bermuda
5. Windward Passage I, Johnson, USA
6. Midnight Sun, Jan Pehrsson, Sweden
7. Ondine V, Huey Long, England
8. Ondine VI, Huey Long, England

Porto Cervo
1. Kialoa IV, John B. Kilroy, USA
2. Helisara, Herbert von Karajan, France
3. Nirvana, Marvin Green, USA
4. Condor, Robert Bell, Bermuda
5. Windward Passage I, Johnson, USA
6. Midnight Sun, Jan Pehrsson, Sweden
7. Ondine V, Huey Long, England
8. Ondine VI, Huey Long, England
9. Il Moro di Venezia I, Raul Gardini, Italy

1983 World Champion
1. Kialoa IV, John B. Kilroy, USA

1984 SORC
1. Kialoa IV, John B. Kilroy, USA
2. Windward Passage I, Johnson, USA
3. Congere, Bevin Koeppel, USA
4. Sorcery, Jacob D. Wood, USA
5. Ondine, Huey Long, England
6. Boomerang, George Coumantaros, USA

Hawaii PanAmClipper Cup*
1. Boomerang, George Coumantaros, USA
2. Kialoa IV, John B. Kilroy, USA
3. Sorcery, Jacob D. Wood, USA
4. Nirvana, Marvin Green, USA
5. Condor, Robert Bell, Bermuda
6. Ragamuffin, Syd Fischer, Australia
7. Winterhawk, Harold Day, USA

St. Francis Perpetual Series*
1. Boomerang, George Coumantaros, USA
2. Kialoa IV, John B. Kilroy, USA
3. Sorcery, Jacob D. Wood, USA
4. Nirvana, Marvin Green, USA
5. Winterhawk, Harold Day, USA
6. Ondine, Huey Long, England

China Sea and Australia Races
Kialoa IV, Condor

1985 SORC
1. Boomerang, George Coumantaros, USA
2. Kialoa IV, John B. Kilroy, USA
3. Matador, William Koch, USA

1985 World Champion — Porto Cervo
1. Boomerang, George Coumantaros, USA
2. Il Moro di Venezia II, Raul Gardini, Italy
3. Emeraude, Jacques Dewailly, France
4. Matador, William Koch, USA
5. Gitana VI, Rothschild, France
6. Kialoa IV, John B. Kilroy, USA
7. Helisara VI, Herbert von Karajan, France
8. Inspiration, Herbert Dahm, West-Germany
9. Cisne Branco, Ribeiro Taves, Navy, Brazil

1986 SORC*
1. Emeraude, Jacques Dewailly, France
2. Boomerang, George Coumantaros, USA
3. Sassy, E. Russel Schmidt, USA
4. Matador, William Koch, USA
5. Condor, Bob Bell, Bermuda

Newport*
1. Ondine VII, Huey Long, England
2. Boomerang, George Coumantaros, USA
3. Matador, William Koch, USA
4. Kialoa V, John B. Kilroy, USA
5. Obsession, Steve Nichols, USA
6. Condor, Robert Bell, Bermuda

1987 SORC
1. Kialoa V, John B. Kilroy, USA
2. Boomerang, George Coumantaros, USA
3. Matador, William Koch, USA
4. Obsession, Steve Nichols, USA
5. UBS Switzerland, Pierre Fehlmann, Switzerland
6. Il Moro di Venezia, Raul Gardini, Italy
7. Ondine VII, Huey Long, England
8. Winterhawk, Harold Day, USA
9. Milene V, Albert Mirlesse, England

Newport
1. Kialoa V, John B. Kilroy, USA
2. Matador, William Koch, USA
3. Ondine VII, Huey Long, USA
4. Boomerang, George Coumantaros, USA
5. Il Moro di Venezia II, Raul Gardini, Italy
6. Emeraude, Jacques Dewailly, France
7. Cannonball, Charles Robertson, USA
8. Obsession, Stephen Nichols, USA
9. Milene V, Albert Mirlesse, England

Porto Cervo
1. Kialoa V, John B. Kilroy, USA
2. Emeraude, Jacques Dewailly, France
3. Il Moro di Venezia III, Raul Gardini, Italy
4. Matador, William Koch, USA
5. Ondine VII, Huey Long, England
6. Othello, Gianni Varasi, Italy
7. Boomerang, George Coumantaros, USA
8. Milene V, Albert Mirlesse, France
9. Inspiration, Herbert Dahm, West-Germany

1987 World Champion (IOR 70.00')
1. Kialoa V, John B. Kilroy, USA
2. Matador, William Koch, USA
3. Il Moro di Venezia III, Raul Gardini, Italy
4. Ondine of Larchmont, Huey Long, England
5. Boomerang, George Coumantaros, USA
6. Milene V, Albert Mirlesse, France

World Champion (IOR 62.50)
1. Emeraude, Jacques Dewailly, France
2. Othello, Gianni Varasi, Italy
3. Cannonball, Charles Robertson, USA
4. Obsession, Stephen Nichols, USA
5. Inspiration, Herbert Dahm, West-Germany

1988 St. Thomas
1. Kialoa V, John B. Kilroy, USA
2. Il Moro di Venezia III, Raul Gardini, Italy
3. Matador, William Koch, USA
4. Emeraude, Jacques Dewailly, France
5. Milene V, Albert Mirlesse, England
6. Ondine VII, Huey Long, England
7. Congere, Bevin Koeppel, USA
8. Inspiration, Herbert Dahm, West-Germany

Kenwood Cup — Hawaii
1. Windward Passage II, Rod Muir, Australia
2. Matador, William Koch, USA
3. Winterhawk, Hal Day, USA
4. Sorcery, Jacob D. Wood, USA
5. Il Moro di Venezia III, Raul Gardini, Italy
6. Sovereign, Bernard Lewis, Australia
7. Congere, Bevin Koeppel, USA
8. Emeraude, Jacques Dewailly, France
9. Ragamuffin, Syd Fischer, Australia
10. Ondine VII, Huey Long, England

St. Francis
1. Il Moro di Venezia III, Raul Gardini, Italy
2. Windward Passage II, Rod Muir, Australia
3. Kialoa V, John B. Kilroy, USA
4. Boomerang, George Coumantaros, USA
5. Emeraude, Jacques Dewailly, France
6. Sovereign, Bernard Lewis, Australia
7. Sorcery, Jacob Wood, USA
8. Matador, William Koch, USA
9. Congere, Bevin Koeppel, USA

1988 World Champion
1. Il Moro di Venezia III, Raul Gardini, Italy
2. Matador, William I. Koch, USA
3. Kialoa V, John B. Kilroy, USA
4. Emeraude, Jacques Dewailly, France
5. Ondine VII, Huey Long, England
6. Congere, Bevin Koeppel, USA
7. Milene V, Albert Mirlesse, England
8. Boomerang, George Coumantaros, USA
9. Inspiration, Herbert Dahm, West-Germany

1989 St. Thomas*
1. Sovereign, Bernard Lewis, Australia
2. Boomerang, George Coumantaros, USA
3. Kialoa V, John B. Kilroy, USA
4. Matador, William Koch, USA
5. Merit, Pierre Fehlmann, Switzerland
6. Congere, Bevin Koeppel, USA
7. NCB Ireland, Bobby Campell, Ireland
8. Milene V, Albert Mirlesse, England

Newport*
1. Sovereign, Bernard Lewis, Australia
2. Emeraude, Jacques Dewailly, France
3. Boomerang, George Coumantaros, USA
4. Kialoa V, John B. Kilroy, USA
5. Matador, William Koch, USA
6. Congere, Bevin Koeppel, USA

Mallorca
1. Longobarda, Gianni Varasi, Italy
2. Il Moro di Venezia III, Raul Gardini, Italy
3. Hispania, Spanish Navy, Spain
4. Drumbeat, Alan Bond, Australia
5. Emeraude, Jacques Dewailly, France
6. Kialoa V, John B. Kilroy, USA
7. Boomerang, George Coumantaros, USA
8. Carmen di Bellavista, Vittorio Moretti, Italy
9. Ondine VII, Huey Long, England
10. Milene V, Albert Mirlesse, England
11. Divirona V, Thierry Tuffier, France

Porto Cervo
1. Longobarda, Gianni Varasi, Italy
2. Il Moro di Venezia III, Raul Gardini, Italy
3. Drumbeat, Alan Bond, Australia
4. Emeraude, Jacques Dewailly, France
5. Kialoa V, John B. Kilroy, USA
6. Hispania, Spanish Navy, Spain
7. Ondine VII, Huey Long, England
8. Carmen di Bellavista, Vittorio Moretti, Italy
9. Milene V, Albert Mirlesse, England
10. Congere, Bevin Koeppel, USA
11. Boomerang, George Coumantaros, USA

St. Tropez
1. Longobarda, Gianni Varasi, Italy
2. Il Moro di Venezia III, Raul Gardini, Italy
3. Hispania, Spanish Navy, Spain
4. Kialoa V, John B. Kilroy, USA
5. Emeraude, Jacques Dewailly, France
6. Ondine VII, Huey Long, USA
7. Carmen di Bellavista, Vittorio Moretti, Italy
8. Milene V, Albert Mirlesse, France
9. Divirona V, Thierry Tuffier, France

Cruising Class
1. Inspiration, Herbert Dahm, West-Germany
2. Speedy Go, V. Gattardo, Monaco

1989 World Champion
1. Longobarda, Gianni Varasi, Italy
2. Il Moro di Venezia, Raul Gardini, Italy
3. Hispania, Spanish Navy, Spain
4. Kialoa V, John B. Kilroy, USA
5. Emeraude, Jacques Dewailly, France
6. Drumbeat, Alan Bond, Australia
7. Ondine VII, Huey Long, England
8. Carmen di Bellavista, Vittorio Moretti, Italy
9. Milene V, Albert Mirlesse, England
10. Boomerang, George Coumantaros, USA
11. Congere, Bevin Koeppel, USA
12. Divirona V, Thierry Tuffier, France

A. Longobarda owner Gianni Varasi with his wife, surrounded by trophies from a successful summer — 1989 World Championship, 1st place winner in Mallorca, Sardinia, and St. Tropez.

B. Longobarda crew and Varasi children celebrate their 1989 victories.

C. Sailing Master Paul Cayard accepting second place trophies for Il Moro di Venezia.

D. Sailing Master Juan Carlos Rodriguez accepting third place trophy for Hispania.

A.

Race Results

Whitbread
Round the World Race

The History

Sailing around the world is a challenge that many yachtsmen aspire to. Racing around the world is the ultimate expression of that aspiration. Round the world sailing and racing are in the same realm as climbing the highest mountain, flying around the globe and all those feats which test man's destiny.

Joshua Slocum captured the attention and the imagination of sailors and sailing enthusiasts everywhere when he completed his 46,000 mile round the world voyage at the turn of the century aboard his yacht *Spray*. The ingenuity and resourcefulness he displayed are prerequisites to the challenge of sailing around the world.

In 1924, the Irishman Connor O'Brien and his crew of two sailed around the world in his 42-foot cutter, *Saiorse*. Vito Dumas' single-handed circumnavigation, in 1942, took l3 months to complete. His ketch, *Lehg II*, was 31 feet long. In 1966, Sir Francis Chichester broke long-standing records when he sailed *Gipsy Moth IV* around the route used by the wool clippers 100 years before. The voyage from Plymouth to Sydney took 107 days, and Chichester completed the return in 119 days. The following year, Sir Alec Rose followed Chichester's route, completing his single-handed voyage in less than a year.

The first actual round the world race was proposed by the London *Sunday Times* in 1967, which offered £5,000 for the fastest nonstop single-handed voyage. The participants could sail from any port on any date prior to October 31, 1968. This Golden Globe Race attracted nine yachts. Only Robin Knox-Johnston, aboard his yacht *Suhaili*, completed the course and received the prize.

The following year, in 1969, two Englishmen, Anthony Churchill, a publisher of a yachting magazine, and Guy Pearse, who had earlier helped to organize the Observer Single-handed Transatlantic Race, attempted to organize a race around the world following the old clipper-ship routes, with stops in Cape Town, Sydney and Rio de Janeiro. They generated a lot of enthusiasm but were unable to raise enough money to hold the event.

In 1972, still with no sponsor, Churchill and Pearse agreed to collaborate with the Royal Naval Sailing Association. Robin Knox-Johnston, a member of the R.N.S.A., along with Flag officer Otto Steiner, believed the time was right for a race round the world for fully crewed yachts. Sir Francis Chichester and Sir Alec Rose joined Knox-Johnston and formed an advisory group. The Whitbread Brewery, which had supported Chichester's voyage, agreed to be the sponsor.

The first Whitbread Round The World Race took place in 1973/74. Seventeen boats made the start. Fourteen yachts from six countries completed the 27,000-mile-course. Although few individuals could take on the expenses of such a campaign, the yachts racing the first Whitbread were totally privately funded.

Mostly cruising yachts participated in the l973/74 race, with the exception of *Great Britain II*, the fastest yacht of all; on corrected time, however, the winner was the Sparkman & Stephens-designed Swan 65 from Mexico, *Sayula II*.

Pacific Ocean

Prevailing Westerlies ▶

Southern Ocean

Leg 1. — Start 2 Sept. '89
                 Arrive Punta Del Este 9-18 Oct.
Leg 2. — Start 28 Oct. Arrive Fremantle 29 Nov.-10 Dec.
Leg 3. — Start 23 Dec. Arrive Auckland 12-16 Jan. '90.
Leg 4. — Start 4 Feb. Arrive Punta Del Este 28 Feb.-8 Mar.
Leg 5. — Start 17 Mar. Arrive Fort Lauderdale 13-21 Mar.
Leg 6. — Start 5 May Arrive Southampton 21-29 May.

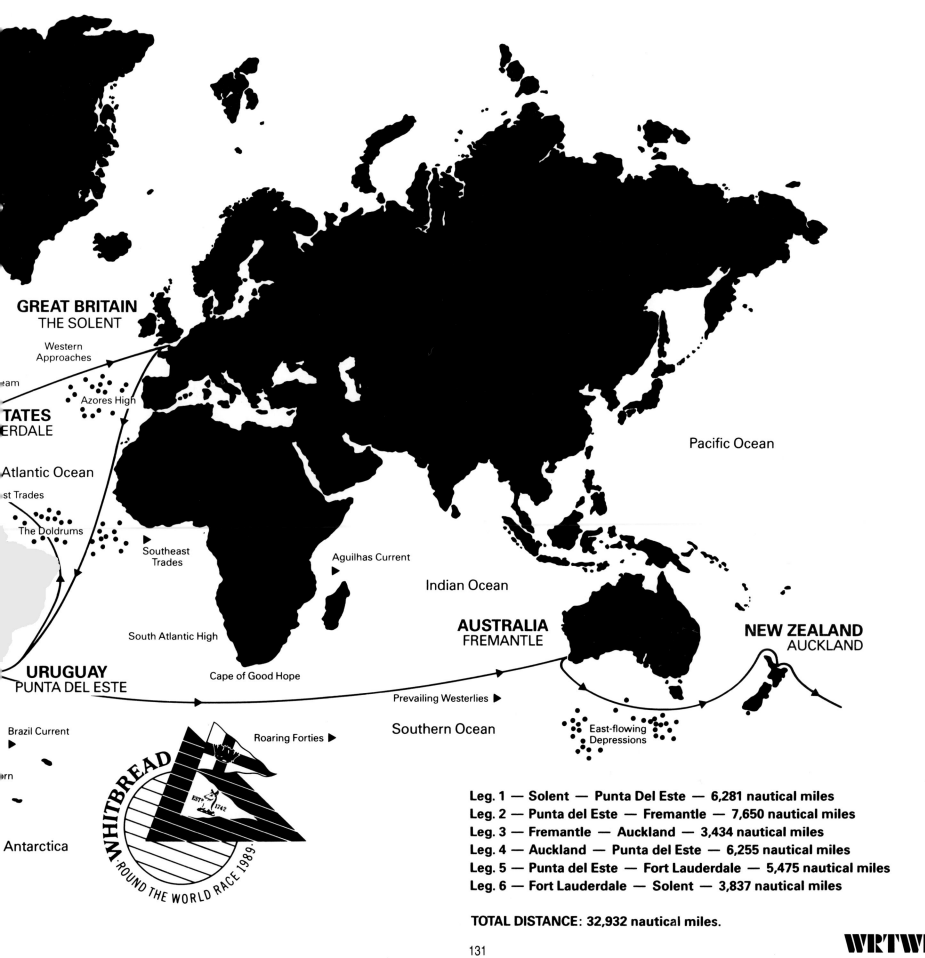

GREAT BRITAIN
THE SOLENT

Western
Approaches

am

TATES
ERDALE

Azores High

Pacific Ocean

Atlantic Ocean

st Trades

The Doldrums

Southeast
Trades

Aguilhas Current

Indian Ocean

South Atlantic High

AUSTRALIA
FREMANTLE

NEW ZEALAND
AUCKLAND

URUGUAY
PUNTA DEL ESTE

Cape of Good Hope

Prevailing Westerlies ▶

Brazil Current

Roaring Forties ▶

Southern Ocean

East-flowing
Depressions

rn

WHITBREAD
ESTd 1742
ROUND THE WORLD RACE 1989

Antarctica

Leg. 1 — Solent — Punta Del Este — 6,281 nautical miles
Leg. 2 — Punta del Este — Fremantle — 7,650 nautical miles
Leg. 3 — Fremantle — Auckland — 3,434 nautical miles
Leg. 4 — Auckland — Punta del Este — 6,255 nautical miles
Leg. 5 — Punta del Este — Fort Lauderdale — 5,475 nautical miles
Leg. 6 — Fort Lauderdale — Solent — 3,837 nautical miles

TOTAL DISTANCE: 32,932 nautical miles.

WRTWR

In the 1977/78 Race, Cornelis van Rietschoten from Holland entered his specially designed ketch *Flyer* which he hoped would win on handicap, and indeed she did. Still, the yacht that made headlines was the one that was the fastest, *Great Britain II*.

The first time that most of the participating yachts were built for the express purpose of participating in the Round the World Race was 1981/82. Notable was "Conny" van Rietschoten's new 76-foot *Flyer*. She had extremely stiff competition from the 67-foot *Ceramco New Zealand* in taking line honors. Unfortunately, *Ceramco* broke her mast on the first leg, forfeiting her chance to win; even so, she was the fastest yacht on corrected time for the rest of race. *Flyer* took the "Double" by winning both on corrected and elapsed time. *Great Britain II*, renamed *United Friendly*, once again performed competitively.

In 1985/86 there was a whole new fleet of racing yachts competing both for handicap and line honors. These yachts were built for the high winds of the Southern Ocean — *Ceramco had* clocked 33 knots surfing four years before. This time, however, it was quite different. Terrible weather greeted the boats as they arrived in Cape Town. *Atlantic Privateer*, leading by 48 hours, broke her mast. Other accidents included serious delamination problems on board *Drum* and *Cote D'Or*.

The rest of the race, characterized by head winds, was relatively uneventful. *Lion New Zealand* had some difficulties with whales, resulting in rudder problems 250 nautical miles before her arrival in Auckland. Despite steering problems, her arrival speed in Auckland harbor was 14 knots! The winner on corrected time was *L'Esprit D'Equipe* that had participated in the last race as *33 Export*. On elapsed time *UBS Switzerland* was the winner.

For the fourth time *Great Britain II* participated in a Whitbread Race, this time under the name *Norsk Data*; she managed to beat her own record by a significant amount of time. It was actually her fifth race around the world, since she had also raced in and won the *Financial Times* Clipper Race, a one-stop race back in 1974.

Over the years the course has changed. The first Whitbread started in Portsmouth, England and went from there to Cape Town, South Africa, Sydney, Australia; then round Cape Horn to Rio de Janeiro, Brazil, and back to Portsmouth. In 1977/78 Sydney was replaced with Auckland, New Zealand, in order to make the two middle legs more even in length, and in 1981/82, Rio de Janeiro was replaced with Mar del Plata, Argentina. In 1985/86 Mar del Plata was exchanged with Punta del Este, Uruguay, due to the Falklands War between Argentina and England.

The course was completely reorganized for the 1989/90 race — from four legs to six and from 27,000 to 32,900 nautical miles. The itinerary included: Southampton, UK — Punta del Este, Uruguay — Perth, Australia — Auckland, New Zealand - Punta del Este, Uruguay — Fort Lauderdale, USA — Portsmouth, UK.

What has never changed, throughout the evolution of the Whitbread, is the challenge it offers to the fortunate few who sail it, the dedication it requires of them, and the excitement it gives to the many who vicariously live it.

BEKEN OF COWES, INC.

ROGER LEAN-VERCOE

Great Britain II *has raced five times around the world under four different names.*

Flyer *was the first yacht to win a race on both elapsed time and on handicap. Now that the IOR rule has changed, it is no longer possible to win the "double."*

UBS Switzerland *was the winner of the 1985/86 Whitbread Race.*

Maiden *was the first yacht to enter the WRTWR with an all-female crew, which included women from Britain, Ireland, France, the United States, and New Zealand. Tracy Edwards, the 27-year-old British skipper, was the only member who had been around the world before. She sold her house to raise cash to buy and prepare the boat, but it wasn't until Royal Jordanian Airlines decided to sponsor* Maiden *that the project became a reality.* Maiden *ran an extremely competitive campaign and Edwards was voted British Yachtsman of the Year (1990).*

Cooking on Board

Napoleon had it right all along — without food and drink the heroes do not last very long at all. (What he actually said was: "An army marches on its stomach.") A cook on board any Whitbread racer is the master of crew comfort, just as the skipper is the master of the yacht's performance.

A seagoing cook needs more than the mere ability to prepare a proper meal. A sense of humor is essential, as the yacht's cook traditionally is the target of a disproportionate amount of teasing and joking. And, as the practitioner of the only vaguely domestic activity on board, the cook acquires the role of confidant and dispenser of philosophy.

Aboard almost all of the Whitbread contenders one person had the cook's job. Very few boats relied on volunteers to handle cooking chores. The top boats were all dependent on freeze-dried food.

On board *Merit*, Zig — Jean Pierre Ziegert — planned all the meals before the start of each leg. A few days before the actual start he explored the local markets and bakeries for fresh food to supplement the freeze-dried meals for the first two weeks or so. On *Fisher & Paykel* a small refrigerator allowed cook Steve Trevurza to bring along a few days' supply of fresh food, while on *Steinlager 2* there was no refrigeration at all, so Cole Sheehan, the cook, worked hard at

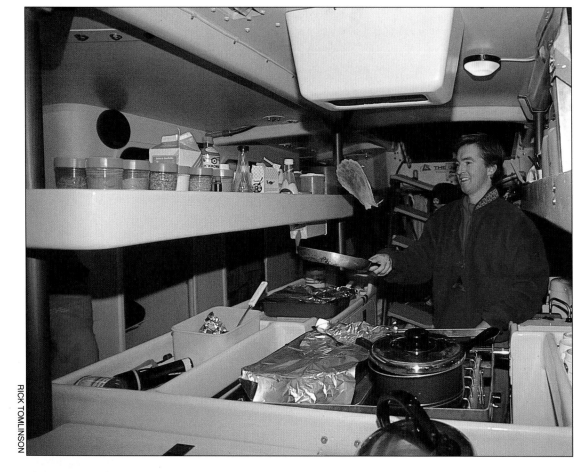

making the freeze-dried rations as interesting as possible.

In the constant effort to save weight, the only wood one finds on a Whitbread maxi is the cook's cutting board. Normally taking weight off a boat's structure simply requires adding money to the budget. Below decks, however, weight is saved by eliminating anything not absolutely necessary. *Steinlager 2* has only one toilet, no shower, no drying facilities, no heating, and no refrigeration. Her skipper, Peter Blake, said that the only thing they really missed on the fifth leg of the 1990 Whitbread (from Punta del Este, Uruguay to Fort Lauderdale, Florida) was a cold drink!

The only new maxi which carried a gimballed table was *Merit*. Pierre Fehlmann, her skipper, insisted on it for the crew's comfort. The crew is organized on a three-watch system, and it took nine 30-minute seatings to feed them three meals a day. Her carefully packed and labeled food inventory included: 40 kilos (88 lbs.) of pasta, 36 kilos (80 lbs.) of rice, 400 fresh and 300 freeze-dried eggs, 21 kilos (46 lbs.) of mashed potato flakes, milk, bread, 40 kilos (88 lbs.) of Swiss cheese... in all, more than 1,000 kilos (2,200 lbs.) of food. The Italian boat *Gatorade* took a lot of pasta and had the luxury of an ice cream machine on board. *Fisher & Paykel*'s cook developed a system of packing all the ingredients needed for two or three days' meals in one plastic box. Each numbered box was brought forward to the galley as needed, and sent aft for storage when empty.

Accidents in the galley can be among the worst that can happen aboard racing yachts. In past races the ship's doctor frequently had to treat the cook for second degree burns or major cuts. Laying out a safe galley takes extensive planning: Everything must be within easy reach, the stove must be gimballed, and the cook have enough room to function, yet be sufficiently restrained and secure in heavy weather, preferably without relying on a galley belt.

Each maxi owns at least one container which is shipped from event to event, or from port to port. Most boats have two containers of duplicate equipment which they alternate, since often the shipping takes longer than the interval between regattas or a leg of the Whitbread race. The containers are filled with sails, rope, rigging materials, all kinds of tools, crew uniforms, and necessary spare parts. Whitbread yachts also ship supplies of freeze-dried food from port to port to ensure its availability.

ICAYA maxis do not ship food, and carry minimal supplies, since the crew lives ashore in apartments or hotels. The yacht manager, who is also responsible for being sure the boat has a full complement of crew, books shore accommodations months in advance. ICAYA crews only carry their own foul weather gear on board for racing. Whitbread crews are limited to very few personal items, and much of their clothing and gear is provided for them. To save weight *Steinlager 2* carried three communal cameras for the crew's use; the number of cassette tapes was limited, and the titles were controlled ahead of time so they did not end up with 15 copies of the same tape!

RICK TOMLINSON

Safety at Sea

Ever since men have been going to sea, their major, fundamental concern has been to keep from being lost overboard. The shout "Man overboard!" is still the most feared by all sailors. All crew members work the boat with the awareness of this danger in the back of their minds, and skippers have a very real responsibility in training the crew in all proper man overboard procedures.

In the first Whitbread Round the World Race (1973/74) the safety gear used was mostly developed for cruising, since the equipment available from merchant marines or navies was either too bulky or inadequate for ocean racing. Foul weather clothing was impractical for the intense activity required in modern blue water racing.

The lessons learned from offshore events such as the Whitbread have spurred the development of new safety gear, and pushed the evolution of existing items.

Three lives were lost during the first Whitbread. Corporal Paul Waterhouse fell overboard from the Italian yawl *Tauranga* on the second leg, approximately 1,500 miles from Cape Town. Four days later, on the same leg, Dominique Guillett, co-skipper of the French boat *33 Export,* was lost overboard. The next leg, from Sidney to Rio de Janeiro, also claimed a casualty when Private Bernard Hoskins fell overboard from *Great Britain II* and drowned in the icy water. In all three cases there were strong winds and high seas, a combination which made it impossible to locate and rescue the victims.

Participants in the Whitbread know that it takes as long as 10 to 12 minutes to turn around an ocean racer sailing at 20 knots in strong winds. The spinnaker must be doused, the main reefed for sailing upwind, and there is always the danger that someone may get injured while carrying out these emergency maneuvers.

During the most recent Whitbread (1989/90) seven sailors fell overboard during the second leg in the Southern Ocean. Of these, six were immediately located and rescued. The seventh, Anthony Phillips from *Creightons Naturally*, drowned, presumably because when he was washed overboard his head hit a stanchion, he was knocked unconscious and therefore unable to activate his life jacket or his Emergency Position Indicating Radio Beacon (EPIRB). Another rescue, of Bart Van Den Dwey, took 30 minutes, which he endured in water as cold as 7° Celsius (36° F). None of the seven involved in these rescues were wearing any special clothing other than normal foul weather gear.

All the information published about hypothermia maintains that a person cannot survive for more than five to eight minutes in water with a temperature of around 5° Celsius (35° F). One of the reasons suggested to explain the survival of these men is that the human body reacts differently to a life-threatening situation than it will in a bath packed with ice with doctors all around.

The six crew members successfully rescued were all carrying personal location transmitters, used for the first time in the Whitbread

WRTWR

race. The radio signal from the transmitter has a range of approximately four miles, and is received by a special radio direction finding system which computes the course to steer back to the lost person. The system was optional for this race, although it will be mandatory in future Whitbreads. Many competitors rushed to purchase these systems in Fremantle, Australia, after they proved their value in the second leg of the race.

For the past three Whitbread races all entries have carried on board the Argos satellite location system, which tracks each yacht and pinpoints its location in case of emergency.

The old type of safety harnesses, which were basically just a belt and a rope tether, have been replaced by nylon webbing, worn around the chest and shoulders to reduce the possibility of back injuries. A short tether and clip allow the crew to secure themselves to deck fittings or wire safety lines running fore and aft on deck.

Whether an evolution of an old design or a new application of modern technology, the new safety gear has contributed enormously to keeping the sport of ocean racing as accident-free as possible, and has brought greater effectiveness to the traditional adage "One hand for the ship and one hand for yourself."

A. There's a place for everything and everything has...
B. Packing the spinnaker
C. Weeks' worth of garbage makes good ballast?
D. Roomy accommodations for Bill and Roger on board The Card
E. Sail loft at sea

A

B

DANIEL FORSTER

136

C

D

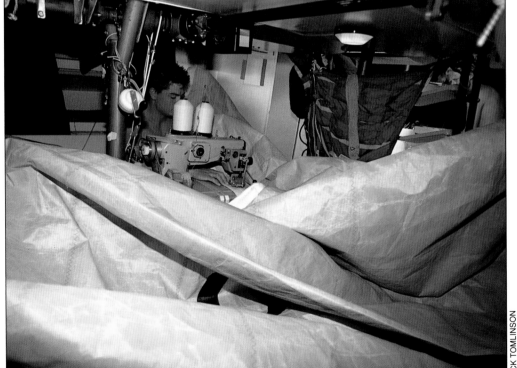

E

WRTWR

A.

Around the World on Grit and Grind...The Whitbread Crew

There are few sporting events tougher than long-distance ocean racing. Crewing on a maxi yacht demands dedication, stamina and courage in conditions that would overwhelm lesser mortals. It means months of battling stormy oceans, rounding notorious landmarks like Cape Horn, and coaxing an unpredictable pace from a boat in the frustration of the mid-Atlantic Doldrums.

These, and other extraordinary challenges, were met by the 300-325 crewmembers who participated in the 1989/90 Whitbread Race. All were determined to do their utmost in the six-leg venture over a period of nine months.

Designers focus on boat performance, and as a result, below decks the boats are quite spartan and extremely cramped. There is no privacy, no way of shutting the door on work and turning to relaxation. Few of the yachts have a proper table where meals can be eaten, or where the oncoming watch can sit and chat with whomever is coming off watch. In some instances, it isn't unusual to have every surface dripping with condensation in 100% humidity while at other latitudes, the temperature on deck and below falls to freezing.

The unstated prerequisites for becoming a crewmember are so numerous and challenging that it's a wonder anyone signs up! Yet when a skipper advertises for crew, applications come in by the hundreds. The preliminary selection criteria is stringent. The 25-40 candidates chosen in the first round are often required to participate in a series of practice passages and races, after which the skipper makes his final decision, based on technical and human considerations. One crewmember who is inevitably in demand is a doctor who can deal with the cuts, breaks and other mishaps that occur en route. The legs in the Southern Ocean are far away from any outside help, so any medical training is a plus. Skippers also look for sailmakers, engineers, computer technicians,

mechanics, and muscle.

The crew of the Swiss sloop *Merit*, skippered by the 1985/86 winner Pierre Fehlmann, were chosen over a year of hard and constant training prior to the start of the race at Southampton in September, 1989.

Crewmembers are inseparable links in a chain, but at the same time they need to feel autonomous. While personal ideas and methods of working are respected, the goal is integration and teamwork. It is the job of the skipper to maintain a cohesive crew or team. Minor altercations that blow up into undreamed of dimensions could have disastrous repercussions. Professionals experienced in forming crews stress friendship as a means of achieving unity on board. Novices are warmly welcomed and helped to adjust quickly. A clear indicator of acceptance is the bestowal of a nickname, imaginative or funny, and often both.

Specific tasks are assigned. It is crucial that every crewmember is able to depend absolutely on the competence of teammates while performing his job. In this cramped, isolated world, any mistake or negligence is immediately observed by the rest of the crew; however, an ideal crew functions well with each other and learns to accept each other's capabilities and limits.

The crew must learn to fall asleep quickly under any circumstances because one watch sleeps while another is on duty. They have to learn to disregard the constant movement, noise and smells. Only a sudden change of rhythm or some unexpected event can wake the watch below.

Who are the crew? Some are daredevils, out for adventure; others have spent their entire lives working on boats. But all are top sailors, seeking an ideal which they find on board an ocean racing yacht.

B.

C.

D.

E.

A. Rigging repair in Auckland

B. Steinlager 2 *Captain Peter Blake preparing for entry into Auckland*

C. Merit *crew muscling the spinnaker*

D. Dining aboard Merit

E. Leg 1 night watch aboard The Card

WRTWR

Belmont Finland II
ex: *UBS Switzerland*

Registry: Finland
Skipper: Harry Harkimo
Sail no. L 8009
Designer: Bruce Farr
Builder: Decision SA- Morges
Year: 1985
IOR-rating: 70.0'
LOA: 24.5m/ 80.38'
LWL: 19.16m/ 62.86'
Beam: 5.63m/ 18.47'
Draft: 4.08m/ 13.39'
Displ: 28,917kg/ 63,750lbs.
Sail loft: WB-Sails
Mainsail: 180m/ 1,937.6sq.ft.
Headsail: 157m/ 1,690sq.ft.
Spinnaker: 289m/ 3,111sq.ft.
Winches: Lewmar/Barbarossa
Mast/rig type: Marechal/fractional
Construction material: FRP composite
Construction method: Vacuum bagged
Engine: Volvo TAM D 30
Generator: Volvo 2001
Desalinator: yes
Electronics: Philips Personal Monitor
  Feedback Weather Satellite Receiver WSR524C
  A.P. Navigator
  Pakratt 232
  0-777 Tono Communications Terminal
  Radio Ocean Radiotelephone RO 1955 MK4
  GME Satnav 310
  Skanti SSB Radiotelephone TRP8250S
  Furuno Radar GaAs
  B&G Homer 5
  B&G Hercules Depthsounder
  B&G Hercules System 390
  Navstar 603S Transit Satellite Navigator
  B&G Distance & Angle Off Course
   Mark 2 Hadrian
  Apple Macintosh SE/30 PC
  Writemove Printer
  Hurta IS/ADB Input System

Skipper: Harry Harkimo

Personal: 36-years-old, married.

Professional Background: Studied economics. Worked as sales manager for a boatyard in Finland.

Sailing Background: Started on Optimist dinghies as a child, then moved on to 505's and 470's. Eventually moved up to half-tonners and 3/4 tonners. Sailed the BOC (single-handed round the world race) and was sailtrimmer on *Skopbank* of Finland in the 1981/82 Whitbread.

Nautical Miles Logged: Approximately 100,000

Best Sailing Experience: The Single-Handed Round the World Race in 1985/86 — "You can prove to yourself that you can do something by yourself...the greatest experience that I will ever have in yachting."

Worst Experience: The Single-Handed Round the World Race. Fell overboard when the boat rolled!

About *Belmont Finland II*: "*UBS Switzerland* was available, and provided a good opportunity for me to start sailing maxis and not have to put in that much money because you don't have a chance to win the race when you are a first-time skipper. You should not spend that much money on a race like this if you do not have a chance to win. The boat needs to be strong so that you know you will get around the world. You learn a lot of things."

About Crew: Mostly Finnish dinghy sailors. Two Soling world champions and several Olympic 470 sailors were on board.

Future: No plans. The boat goes back to the owner after the Whitbread.

Belmont Finland II

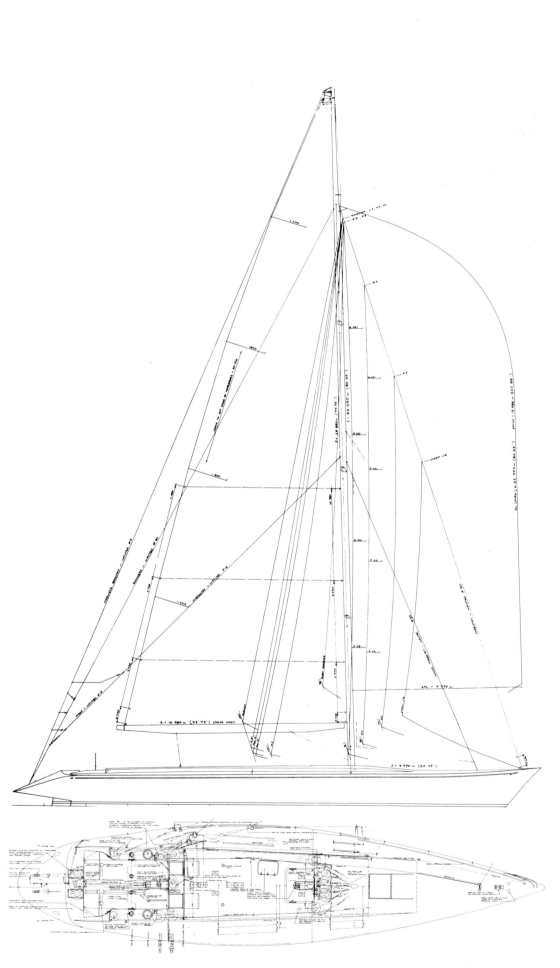

According to Bruce Farr and those in the know, an old maxi like the ex UBS Switzerland, *winner of WRTWR 1985/86, was bound to be slower than the new maxis by at least 1%. Still, Harry Harkimo was not prepared for how devastating that 1% would be over 33,000 miles.*

" — I don't want to have a boat like this after the race. Nobody wants to have a maxi boat after the Whitbread race. What do you do with the boat? You have to maintain it, you don't have any sponsors left because the race is over, it costs you a lot of money, it's a big problem to sell it...there are 50 boats for sale after the race."

Harry Harkimo

Belmont Finland II

Charles Jourdan

Skipper: Alain Gabbay

Personal: 35-years-old; one daughter. Born in Egypt, moved to Marseille when young.

Sailing Background: Developed a passion for sailing when living in Marseille. Started on Optimists, then 470's and 505's. Soon moved to larger yachts; had first job as skipper at age 16. First ocean race as skipper was 1976 OSTAR, Jester Trophy; finished 10th overall, 5th in class. Was skipper of 33 Export in 1977/78 Whitbread, won second leg. Signed contract with Charles Heidsieck to race the 1981/82 Whitbread, finishing second on handicap behind *Flyer*. In the early 80's the Charles Heidsieck Company was acquired by a horseman, and stopped sponsoring sailboats.

"I try to earn my living with boats. Sometimes it's very difficult because sometimes I have no money...sometimes it's difficult to try to live with this profession."

Nautical Miles Logged: "I never counted."

Best Sailing Experience: "I have a lot of best experiences."

Worst Experience: Finishing a close second on handicap in the 1981/82 Whitbread. Decided then I would return to the Whitbread on a maxi, race in real time — "never on handicap again!"

About *Charles Jourdan*: "We take another philosophy of the maxi. The rating is 70, but the boat is very light, without too much sail, and not very long. She is not so far from an ULDB, and [she is] approximately half the weight of the other maxis. The overall length is 1.5 meters shorter, the waterline length the same [as the other maxis]. We have a boat made to race downwind, very fast, and we have some problems to have the same speed as the other maxis upwind and reaching. The idea was the designer's. Both the project manager and I agreed that it would be a good idea."

About Crew: All French. There were "three three-man watches, three hours each. The navigator and the skipper don't stand watch. On easy watches, we are three on watch plus the skipper or the navigator. If there is a more difficult situation, the next watch is on standby, which makes eight persons on deck. And for the panic, it's all on deck!"

Future: Race the Globe Challenge. "Now for me it's time to do something on my own without a crew. I very much like to race with a crew because I think human relations are very good. But for my own experience I would like to race once single-handed."

Registry: France
Owner: Sandro Buzzi
Sail no. F 8992
Skipper: Alain Gabbay
Designer: Guy Ribadeau Dumas
Builder: Nordhal MABIRE/MAG
Year: 1989
IOR-rating: 69.5'
LOA: 22m/ 72.18'
LWL: 20.4m/ 66.9'
Beam: 5.29m/ 17.36'
Draft: 3.02m/ 9.84'
Displ: 18,300kg/ 40,344lbs.
Sail loft: North/Voiles Systeme
Mainsail: 145m/ 1,561sq.ft.
Headsail: 105m/ 1,130sq.ft.
Spinnaker: 250m/ 2,691sq.ft.
Winches: Harken/Barbarossa
Mast/rig type: Marechal/fractional
Construction material: Prepeg carbon
Construction method: Vacuum bagged
Engine: Volvo TMD 31
Generator: Maecklink/BMW
Electronics: Furuno DFAX
　Shipmate RS 5100 Satellite Navigator
　Thrane & Thrane TT-3210A Radiotelex Modem
　Koden MD-3000 Radar
　Skanti TRP8750S SSB Radio System
　　Receiver/Transmitter
　NKE Windinstruments-log-speed-
　　logbookprinter
　Navigator LRX 322 Loran C Double Chain
　Sailor S.P. Radio Watchkeeping receiver R501
　Macintosh SE/30 PC
　Writemove printer
　NC-77 Calculator

Charles Jourdan

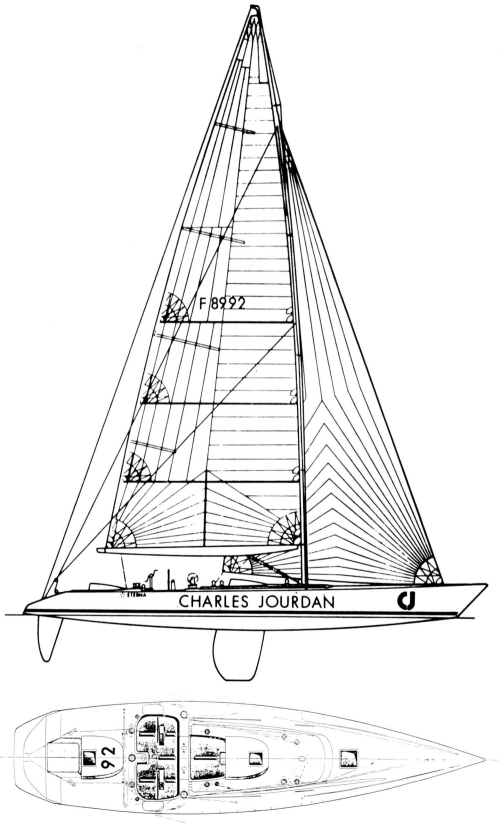

DANIEL FORSTER

 Alain Gabbay, his friend Mario, and the entire crew studied the weather pattern of the Whitbread race course and decided on a downwind design. Therefore, Charles Jourdan was designed similar to an ultra light displacement boat. Unfortunately, there was not as much strong downwind racing as they anticipated.

 Launched late, the first two legs of the race were virtually a sea trial. It was not until the third leg of the race that she was able to prove her prowess downwind. She was in the lead when suddenly she was hit by a whale! The impact delaminated the port side. As the cook said, "I was preparing lunch below deck when I heard a big bang and suddenly saw the light."

Charles Jourdan

Fazisi

Fazisi made a big splash as the first maxi from the USSR ever to enter the Whitbread. Arriving late on the scene, she seemed plagued from the start. Flown from the Soviet Union in an Air Force plane to London/Heathrow Airport, Fazisi was transported by lorry to Hamble River where she was finished and launched just a month before the race started. No one anticipated the IOR rating to be almost 73'.

To reduce the rating the forestay was moved aft and the small keel (more appropriate to a 60-footer) was exchanged with Rothman's old one after which her rating came below the 70.05' maximum.

She did surprisingly well on the first leg to Uruguay. Therefore, it was a tragedy and a shock to all when co-skipper Alexei Grischenko committed suicide. Fazisi had been in financial trouble from the start, still she managed to complete the race with the enormous help and support from local people in each port of call.

Fazisi

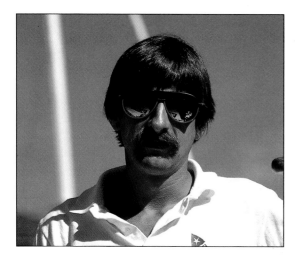

Skipper: Skip Novak

Personal: 37-years-old. From Chicago. Attended University of Florida.

Sailing Background: Has sailed entire life. Sailing professionally since age 22. Left the United States after 1976. Raced 1977/78 Whitbread on *King's Legend*. Decided Europe was the place to be for long-distance sailing. Based in Europe for past 13 years. Sailed 1981/ 82 Whitbread on *Alaska Eagle* and 1985/86 on *Drum* as skipper. Has worked steadily as a delivery skipper. "I am very interested in the traveling aspect of sailing. I am first a traveler, then a sailor. Sailing allows me to travel." Built *Pelagic* in partnership with others. Sailed around Antarctica and Tierra del Fuego for five months. Interested in expedition sailing. Offered to work with Soviet team. Started as project consultant, was eventually voted co-skipper and later became skipper of *Fazisi*.

Nautical Miles Logged: 280,000

Best Sailing Experience: Winning the Parmelia Race on *Independent Endeavour*, a production Swan 65.

Worst Experience: "*Alaska Eagle*...but I don't want to talk about it."

About *Fazisi*: "I joined the project late, after the hull was finished, and helped with the deck and interior layout."

About Crew: Crew selection consisted of choosing among the five best Soviet skippers. Each was asked to make his own preparation plan for the entire race. Had to have this competition because no one in the USSR had any experience in maxis, the biggest boats available being 54'. Also, it gave sailors from various regions the chance to participate in the project. Each candidate brought in his own crew, providing a larger group of qualified people to choose from. Considerable attention was paid to the ability of crew members to work as a team.

Among the crew are people of various technical backgrounds: electrical engineers, mechanics, electronics specialists and doctors. All are good sailors. Several are from the Soviet Olympic team, and others have offshore experience.

Future: Back to Antarctica on *Pelagic*, then the tropics. Want to do less and less racing, more sailing.

Registry: USSR
Skipper: Skip Novak
Sail no. SR 1989
Designer: Mernikov/Design-Group VTK, Poti
Builder: Poti Shipbuilding Plant
Year: 1989
IOR-rating: 70'
LOA: 25.23m/ 82.75'
LWL: 21.37m/ 70.92'
Beam: 5.8m/ 19'
Draft: 3.2m/ 10.5'
Displ: 25,500kg/ 56,217lbs.
Ballast: 10,000kg/ 22,046lbs.
Sail loft: North, West-Germany
Mainsail: 155m/ 1,668sq.ft.'
Headsail: 105m/ 1,130sq.ft.
Spinnaker: 210m/ 2,260.5sq.ft.
Winches: Barient
Mast/rig type: Sparcraft/fractional
Construction material: Aluminum
Construction method: Welded
Electronics: ICOM VHF IC-M100
   ICOM HF IC-M700
   Skanti 400W receiver/transmitter TRP8400S
   Trimble Navigation Loran-GPS 10X
   AP Navigator - Decca
   Magnavox MX4102 Satellite Navigator
   Furuno DFAX
   Furuno radar 1720
   Weathercheck 32 Hour Digital Barograph - Banair
   Ockham System

Fazisi

Fisher & Paykel

Digital readouts of speed and wind instruments help the crew keep the boat moving at top speed.

Registry: New Zealand
Skipper: Grant Dalton
Sail no. KZ-400
Captain: Erle Williams
Designer: Bruce Farr
Builder: Marten Marine Industries, Ltd.
Year: 1988
IOR-rating: 69.97'
LOA: 24.98m/ 81.96'
LWL: 19.9m/ 65.29'
Beam: 5.66m/ 18.57'
Draft: 3.85m/ 12.63'
Displ: 31,914kg/ 70,357lbs.
Sail loft: North
Mainsail: 125m/ 1,346sq.ft.
Headsail: 176m/ 1,895sq.ft.
Spinnaker: 325m/ 3,498sq.ft.
Mizzen: 69m/ 743sq.ft.
Mizzen staysail: 166m/ 1,787sq.ft.
Winches: Lewmar
Mast/rig type: Masthead ketch
Construction material: FRP composite
Construction method: Vacuum bagged
Electronics: Sailor SP Receiver R1119
  Sailor SP Exciter S1303
  Sailor SP Transmitter T1135
  Sailor SP Watchkeeping Receiver R501
  Sailor SP VHF C403
  Furuno DFAX
  Trimble Navigation Loran-GPS 10X
  Magnavox MX4102 Satellite Navigator
  Raytheon R40 Raster Scan Radar
  Zenith Data Systems PC
  A.P. Navigator
  Feedback Weather Satellite Receiver WSR524C
  Diconix 300 Printer
  Data Spec
  Mitsubishi Video Copy Processor
  Banair - Weathercheck Digital Barograph
  Microvax Computer
   with weather routine software
  Digital VT 330 Monitor
  Ockam Boatspeed - Brandstedt Driver
  Ockam Polar Boatspeed - Brandstedt Driver
  Ockam Windspeed True - Brandstedt Driver
  Ockam Windangle True - Brandstedt Driver
  Ockam Wind Angel Apparent
   - Brandstedt Driver
  Ockam Cal Boatspeed Master
  Ockam Cal Windspeed
  Ockam Test Errors

Fisher & Paykel

Skipper: Grant Dalton

Personal: 31-years-old, youngest of three brothers; resides in Auckland. Tried rugby and motorbike racing — and has run in marathons.

Professional Background: University degrees in accountancy. Currently, full-time sailor.

Sailing Background: Started in dinghies, which were hand-me-downs from older brother. Has been sailing full-time since the age of 23. "From the moment I saw *Heath Condor* sail into Auckland Harbor in 1977, I wanted to sail the Whitbread."

Applied to Peter Blake for a position on *Ceramco New Zealand in 1981*, but was cut from that crew. Applied to Flyer and was accepted.

"I applied to *Flyer* early on and got a letter back saying, 'We're full, thanks very much.' I reapplied and I got a telegram back — it was like a Thursday — saying 'Well, we're interested; there are some Dutch people in Auckland who will interview you...can you see them in the next day or two.' I did, and they obviously gave me good reference. That was a Saturday when I saw them, and on Monday I got a telegram saying 'You're on!' and I left on a Wednesday. And I never looked back..."

Nautical Miles Logged: 100,000

Best Sailing Experience: Launching of *Fisher & Paykel*.

Worst Experience: "I've never really had a worst experience."

About Fisher & Paykel: Developed two computer models for the course, one assuming perfect knowledge of weather, the other sailing Great Circle routes. Based on models, they developed two yacht designs which the computer predicted would finish in 140 days.

"Then we said, right, let's do something really radical, and put a ketch rig in her. The ketch came out at a 135 days. So we said, that's interesting, better go out and have a drink, because something is going wrong!

"The question then became whether to believe the numbers, to try to justify what the computer was saying. We developed two boats, a fractional sloop and a ketch, because one of them wasn't right. And the decision was never made until two days before the boat started to be built."

About Crew: 140 applied, 17 were accepted. Used two-watch system because ketch rig needs a lot of people on deck. "I interviewed all because once upon a time someone gave me a break and it's easy to just look at a letter and say no." Crew selected on ability to be totally uncompromising in their desire to win. Compatibility. Helmsmanship ("My experience in the last two races has been that when it's blowing hard you run out of helmsmen very quickly. There are only a few guys who can steer these things.") Trade (doctor and sailmaker of equal appeal).

Future: Perhaps another Whitbread, depending on results of this one. Will keep sailing.

"We found a sponsor in May, 1987. The race was always approached with the objective that if we couldn't get all the money there was no point because the boats that did have all the money were going to beat you."

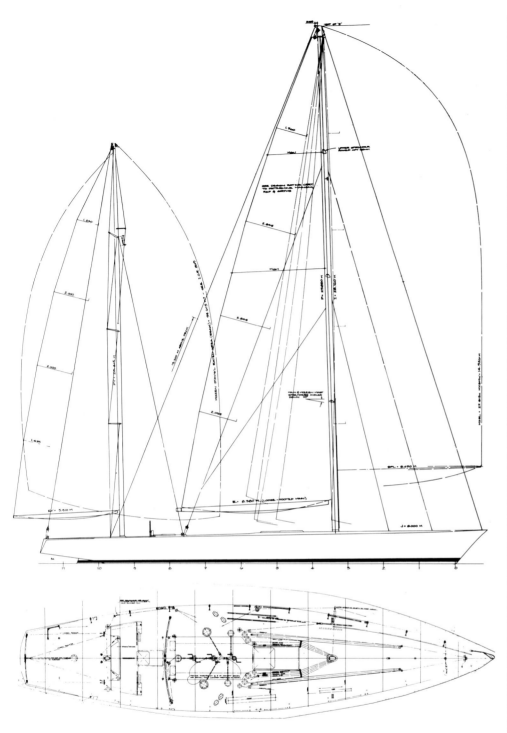

The preparation and planning behind this project is not unlike a highly developed military campaign. What can be controlled is under control. The determination and commitment of the crew is noticeable. Fisher & Paykel perhaps only lacked luck in a few decisive moments.

Editor's Note: Fisher & Paykel *was purchased in the Spring of 1990 by Gianni Varasi.*

Fisher & Paykel

Fortuna Extra Lights

Skipper: Jan Santana

Personal Notes: Age 36. Born in Barcelona. Married, three children. Attended University of Barcelona, studied one year of medicine, three years of economics.

Professional Background: Worked in France at the Stearns spar factory. Currently owns a sailmaking business.

Sailing Background: Started competing in dinghies at age 15, in the Vaurien class, 420's, 470's. Became 1976 Vaurien world champion. Member of Tornado class Olympic team for the 1988 Seoul Games. Won Mediterranean Half-ton championship in 1978. Santana was involved in the first *Fortuna* project for the 1985/86 Whitbread.

Nautical Miles Logged: 50,000

Best Experience: Finishing second in the European half-ton championships.

Worst Experience: The 1979 Fastnet.

About *Fortuna*: Designed specifically to win Whitbread. Javier Visiers (the designer) felt that she needed to be good for winds of 25 knots or better. She is the first maxi yacht conceived, designed, and built entirely in Spain. A thorough study of materials was made to determine the most suitable construction for a very light, strong boat. *Fortuna* was specifically built to withstand the stresses of offshore racing, and to take maximum advantage of the predominant reaching and running conditions.

About Crew: Santana has sailed with all crew members before; looked for character and psychological profile to last for entire race. "When we look for this type of character, we always find it in people with experience, and [therefore] there would never be any new people in ocean racing... For that reason we decided to always take two new people in every ocean race.

"The most delicate and important factor is living together on board. The fastest boat in the world won't win anything if you don't keep in mind the basic principles of respect between crew members."

Remarks: "Ocean races should be taken as a blend of business, adventure and competition; that is to say: with the seriousness of a business, with the acceptance of the risk inherent in any adventure, and with a competitive spirit 24 hours a day."

Registry: Spain
Skipper/ Leg 1,3,4,6: Jan Santana Fuster
Skipper/ Leg 2,5: Javier de la Gandara Alonso
Sail no. E 1992
Designer: Javier Visires Rodriguez
Builder: Visiers de la Rocha-Mefasa Shipyards
Year: 1988
IOR-rating: 69.14'
LOA: 23.55m/ 77.26'
LWL: 18.48m/ 60.63'
Beam: 5.8m/ 19.03'
Draft: 4.05m/ 13.33'
Displ: 23,420kg/ 51,631lbs.
Sail loft: Toni Tio Velas Team
Mainsail: 140m/ 1,507sq.ft.
Headsail: 136m/ 1,464sq.ft.
Spinnaker: 290m/ 3,122sq.ft.
Winches: Lewmar
Mast/rig type: Fractional
Construction material: Composite
Construction method: Vacuum bagged
Electronics: Sailor SP Compact VHF RT2048
 Furuno DFAX FAX-214 Facsimile Receiver
 Furuno Satellite Navigator FSN-50
 Furuno Radar GaAs Fet Front End.
 4-Tone Daylight Display
 B&G Hercules System 390
 Skanti HF-SSB Receiver/Transmitter TRP8750S
 Plus Passport PC - STI Keyboard - STI Monitor
 CRM Oceanide - Radio Beacon Safe System
 Barograph
 Silva 325
 On Deck Computer: Prism- Crain La Rochelle
 Software:Jason
 System for Transoceanic Weather Routing

Fortuna Extra Lights

At the start of the 1988 Discovery Race (tracing Columbus's 496-year-old route to the New World), Santana and Visiers provided strong competition for Merit. Unfortunately, they were not as successful at the start of the Whitbread. Arriving in Fremantle after the second leg, the crew took some hard knocks — one broke a leg, another his collarbone, and a third dislocated his shoulder. Nonetheless, in the next leg the Spaniards excelled once again. They set a new Whitbread record for speed: They managed to cover 398 nautical miles in one day.

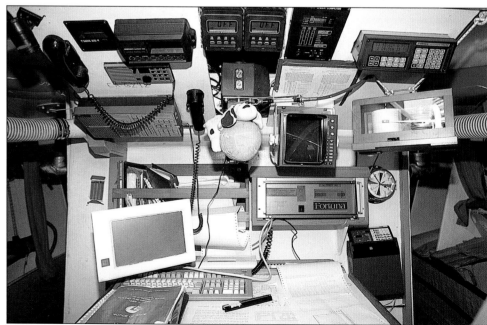

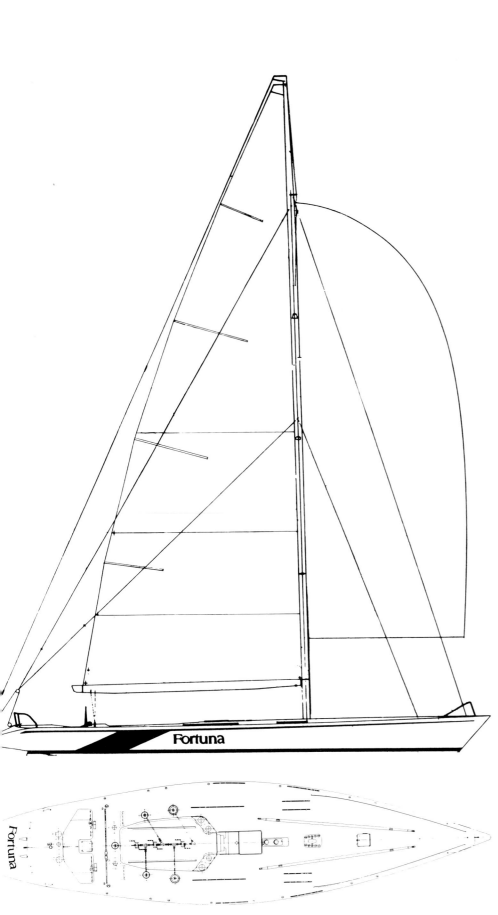

DANIEL FORSTER

Fortuna Extra Lights

Gatorade

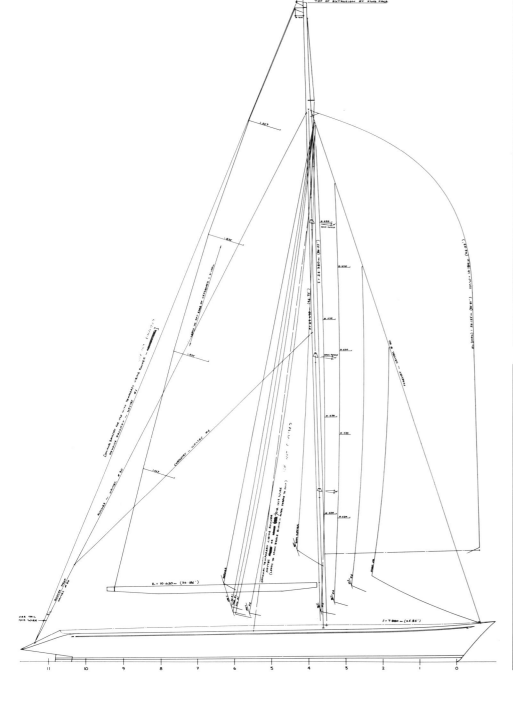

During the 1985/86 Whitbread, when she was NZI Enterprise, *skippered by Digby Taylor,* Gatorade *had an exciting memorable race against* Atlantic Privateer *on their approach to Auckland, New Zealand. After being at sea for 7,100 nautical miles,* Gatorade *lost by a mere eight minutes! Today, despite being a generation older,* Gatorade, *under the guidance of Falck, is racing better than some of the newest maxis.*

Gatorade

Skipper/Owner: Giorgio Falck

Personal: 52-years-old. Has five children and lives in Milan with his wife, Rosanna Schiaffino. Son Giovanni, who recently received engineering degree, was on board for the entire Whitbread.

Professional Background: Nuclear engineer "which I have always had a passion for." Worked in Switzerland before becoming CEO of family-owned steel company.

Sailing Background: Started sailing in Stars when 12-years-old. Sailed one-designs for 15 years. Began racing offshore in 1969. Raced five times in Fastnet Race, six in Sardinia Cup, two in Admiral's Cup. Finished 5th with *Guia IV* in 1973/74 Whitbread. Was 13th out of 29 in 1981/82 Whitbread with *Rolly Go*. Has owned six offshore yachts including *Gatorade*.

Nautical Miles Logged: Approximately 100,000

Best Sailing Experience: The 1973/74 Whitbread Race.

Worst Experience: "Certainly when I learned on the phone that *Guia* had sunk. On the way home from the Cape Town-Rio Race, *Guia* was attacked by a killer whale and sank in less than five minutes. All the crew was picked up after 18 hours in the lifeboat."

About Gatorade: Wanted to do a third Whitbread Race, but budget was limited and time was short. Decided to buy the best used boat — *NZI Enterprise*. After the Discovery Race in 1988, which gave opportunity to test the boat against five other maxis, a lot was changed on board. Installed a new keel (two tons lighter), a new mast, sails and the main engine. Removed all hydraulics to simplify things.

About Crew: All 12 crew on board were amateurs, racing out of passion. "The Southern Ocean demands more. I was aboard on the first, third and fifth legs, as much as my work would allow. Also because in the South you need to be a young crew, and in the other legs you need intelligence."

Future: "I do not know if I will keep *Gatorade*. It is difficult to sail on a smaller boat after sailing a maxi. Maybe I will change her to a cruising boat... I do not know, I have no plans yet. I don't think I will go into ICAYA racing because you need a lot of money — a sponsor is not permitted.

Gatorade

"I think ICAYA is a completely stupid way to utilize a maxi. It is a question of opinion. It is like going to the office with a Rolls Royce or to buy a pack of cigarettes... to race for 25 miles and come back. It is completely another philosophy. For me the number of miles you sail is a more important thing. To sail 25 miles is nothing. A big boat like this — the right utilization is a big race... If you want to race a 25-mile race — sail a J-24!"
Giorgio Falck

Registry: Italy
Skipper: Giorgio Falck
Sail no. I-11441
Captain: Pierre Sicouri
Designer: Bruce Farr
Builder: Digby Taylor
Year: 1985
IOR-rating: 70'
LOA: 24.4m/ 80'
LWL: 19.45m/ 63.75'
Beam: 5.54m/ 18.17'
Draft: 3.81m/ 12.5'
Displ: 27,213kg/ 59,993lbs.
Sail loft: Sobstad
Mainsail: 174m/ 1,873sq.ft.
Headsail: 163m/ 1,754sq.ft.
Spinnaker: 300m/ 3,229sq.ft.
Winches: Barient/barbarossa
Mast/rig type: Marechal/fractional
Construction material: FRP Composite
Construction method: Vacuum bagged
Electronics: Macintosh SE/30 PC
  Writemove Printer
  Hurta IS/ADB Digitalizer
  B&G Hercules 2
  Raytheon V700 Video Echo Sounder
  Kenwood TS-440S HF Transceiver
  Thrane & Thrane Message Terminal
  Thrane & Thrane STD-C Transceiver
  Thrane & Thrane TT3602a Monochrome Display
  Belcom VHF GX552-NZ
  Electro-Nav EN-2182R Watch Receiver
  Furuno Facsimile Receiver FAX-108
  Furuno Satellite Navigator FSN-70
  Furuno Radar GaAs Fet Front End.
   4-Tone Daylight Display
  Skanti 400W Receiver/Transmitter TRP8400S
  JVC Video/Cassette Recorder BR-S410EX
  Magellan GPS NAV 1000 Satellite Navigator
  Barograph

Gatorade

Liverpool Enterprise ex: *Atlantic Privateer*

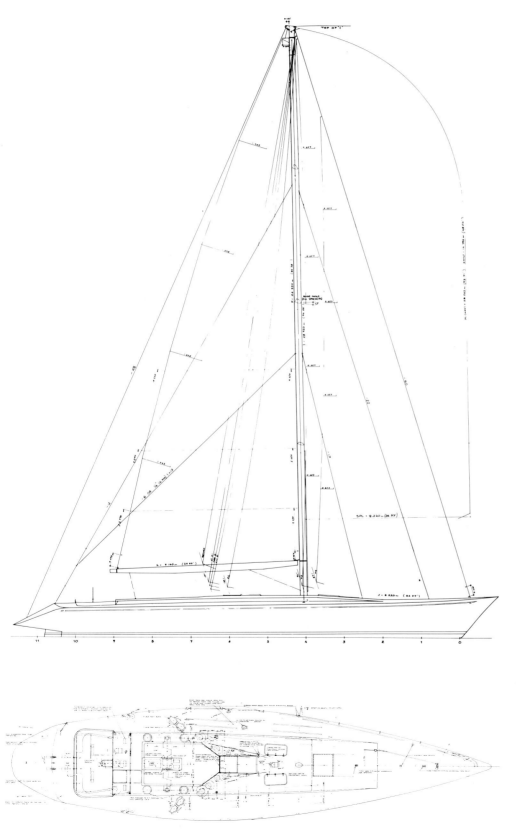

Registry: England
Skipper: Bob Salmon
Sail no. K-696
Designer: Bruce Farr
Builder: RTW Yachts, Inc.
Year: 1984
IOR-rating: 69.5'
LOA: 24.32m/ 79.83'
LWL: 19.25m/ 63.17'
Beam: 5.74m/ 18.83'
Draft: 3.75m/ 12.33'
Displ: 30,332kg/ 66,869lbs.
Sail loft: North
Mainsail: 139m/ 1,496sq.ft
Headsail: 186m/ 2,002sq.ft
Spinnaker: 343m/ 3,692sq.ft.
Winches: Lewmar
Mast/rig type: Rondal/masthead
Construction material: FRP Composite
Construction method: Vacuum bagged
Electronics:
  Seafarer 700 Depth Sounder
  IMR 5500 Mk.2 2182kHz Loudspeaker
   Watch Receiver
  Sailor SP Exciter S1301
  Sailor SP 1200
  Sailor SP Receiver R1117
  Sailor SP N1400
  ICOM IC-720 HF All Band Receiver
  King 8001 Loran
  Racal-Decca Radar
  Toshiba Express Writer 301
  Toshiba 5200 PC
  Skanti VHF TRP2500
  Abby AT PC - Transmit of Video Photo
  Furuno DFAX
  Fusion System 256

Liverpool Enterprise

Formerly Atlantic Privateer, Liverpool Enterprise *was one of the fastest boats in the 1985/86 Whitbread. Unfortunately, due to lack of funding, she was unable to match her previous performance. Bob Salmon and his crew were hesitant to put any pressure on the boat, fearful of the repercussions in the event of any breakage.*

Skipper/Owner: Bob Salmon

Personal: Lives in England. Married, with three children and four grandchildren.

Professional Background: After a career as a photojournalist, became a professional yachtsman. Has been delivering both sail and power yachts for 18 years. Also marine consultant.

Sailing Background: Developed a passion for yachts when covering the first nonstop Single-Handed Round the World Race. In 1972 bought a boat and entered the OSTAR, where he was dismasted in mid-Atlantic. No previous experience on maxis before last Whitbread. "There was no previous [racing] experience, we were still putting the crew and the boat together on the day of the start. Not the way to go racing."

Nautical Miles Logged: Over 350,000

Best Sailing Experience: The first single-handed trip I ever made. When you arrive after completing something like that there is an exhilaration which is almost impossible to compare with anything else. The second one is never as good. You are always trying to relive the first one."

Worst Experience: The commercial pressures associated with the Whitbread campaign. The worst sailing experiences were two dismastings in mid-Atlantic, sinking in the Bay of Biscay, and having a catamaran break up during a Force-9 storm.

About *Liverpool Enterprise*: Seemed to be the only competitive boat on the market. "I borrowed money and bought her, but my sponsors canceled. The local merchants in Liverpool formed a charitable trust to buy the boat after the race."

Future: She will be used as an ocean training vessel.

Remarks: "I was disenchanted with the way international racing was going. It was becoming obvious that victory was only available to those who could find massive funding. Even in those days (1972) OSTAR was becoming too expensive for an ordinary yachtsman. So my wife and I conceived the idea of the Mini-Transat, which is a single-handed transatlantic race for very small yachts. It was, in its early days, very contentious. But my philosophy was that if we limited the size of the yachts to something very small it wouldn't be possible to spend too much money on them. In fact, I was quite wrong. When you go racing, you can spend as much as... The boats very quickly became quite exotic, I mean, carbon fiber shells...it was fascinating as an exercise."

Liverpool Enterprise

Martela O.F.

The fastest of the three Finnish boats, Martela O.F.'s racing career was halted suddenly on February 26, 1990 when the keel fell off. She capsized 330 nautical miles from Punta del Este, Uruguay. None of the crew were injured and only four got wet since the problem with the keel had been common knowledge for the last 36 hours. Four-and-a-half-hours after the capsize, all crew were rescued with five taken on board Charles Jourdan and 11 on board Merit. There was hope that the hull could be towed ashore and then shipped to Fort Lauderdale for repair in due time for the last leg, but weather and other circumstances prevented it.

"Most good ocean racers have small boat background anyway."

Markku Wiikeri

Skipper: Markku Wiikeri

Personal: 36-years-old. Lives in Finland.

Professional Background: After leaving the Navy studied economics in Sweden. Quit college to deliver a Swan 65 to the Caribbean, stayed there sailing for several months. Returned to Finland and started a company importing French boats and yachting hardware. Worked in Northern Finland as sales manager for Advance Yachts.

Sailing background: Started at age five on Optimist dinghies and moved up to small keelboats. Sailed with father on offshore boats from age 14. Raced on many half-tonners and 3/4 tonners. Twice won Finnish half-ton championships.

After 1977 started sailing on larger boats. Was on *Skopbank of Finland* for the 1981/82 Whitbread. Stayed on board *Skopbank* as skipper with new American owner. Sailed the Caribbean and U.S. East Coast extensively. In 1986 started serious maxi project for the Whitbread. Currently professional sailor.

Nautical Miles Logged: 150,000 (not including cruising)

Best Sailing Experience: The Whitbread on *Skopbank* — "...the nice weather in the Southern Ocean!"

Worst Experience: The '85 Fastnet — "Breaking the headfoil on *Colt International* in heavy weather and having to drop out."

About *Martela O.F.*: A conservative boat. Chose German Frers as designer because his ideas were the closest to their requirements, and his designs have dominated round-the-buoys racing. German Frers offered three design alternatives: light, medium, heavy. Chose the medium displacement. Felt the others were too risky.

So far happy with the boat. Raced the Transat from Lorient to St. Barts and back. On the first leg *Merit* beat Martela O.F. by 4 1/2 hours. On the return leg *Merit* beat them by two hours and 15 minutes — "so we're getting better!"

About Crew: My co-skipper, Antero Kairamo, worked with Frers during the design process. 15-16 crew were chosen on the basis of ocean-racing experience. Looked for a good mix of non-sailing skills as well, such as doctors and engineers.

Martela O.F.

Registry: Finland
Skipper: Markku Wiikeri
Co-skipper: Antero Kairamo
Sail no. L 9000
Designer: German Frers
Builder: Baltic Yachts
Year: 1989
IOR-rating: 70.05'
LOA: 24.58m/ 80.65'
LWL: 20m/ 65.6'
Beam: 5.92m/ 19.42'
Draft: 3.9m/ 12.75'
Displ: 29,730kg/ 65,400lbs.
Ballast: 16,513kg/ 36,404lbs.
Sail loft: Hood, Doyle, WB-Sails
Mainsail: 173.78m/ 1,871sq.ft.
Headsail: 162.53m/ 1,750sq.ft.
Spinnaker: 359.78m/ 3,873sq.ft.
Winches: Lewmar
Mast/rig type: Sparcraft/fractional
Construction material: Composite
Construction method: Vacuum bagged
Engine: Cummins 4BT 3.9m
Electronics: Toshiba 1600
  Diconix 150 printer
  Summagraphics
  Barograph Aneros
  Brookes & Gatehouse Hercules
   System 390
  A.P. Navigator
  Navstar 2000 Satellite Navigator
  Low Range LMS-300 Marine System
  Furuno DFAX
  Furuno Navigator FSN-90
  Furuno Radar GaAs color
  SP Sailor Receiver Type R1119
  SP Sailor Exciter Type S1304
  SP Sailor Transmitter Type T1130
  Navico VHF RT 6500S

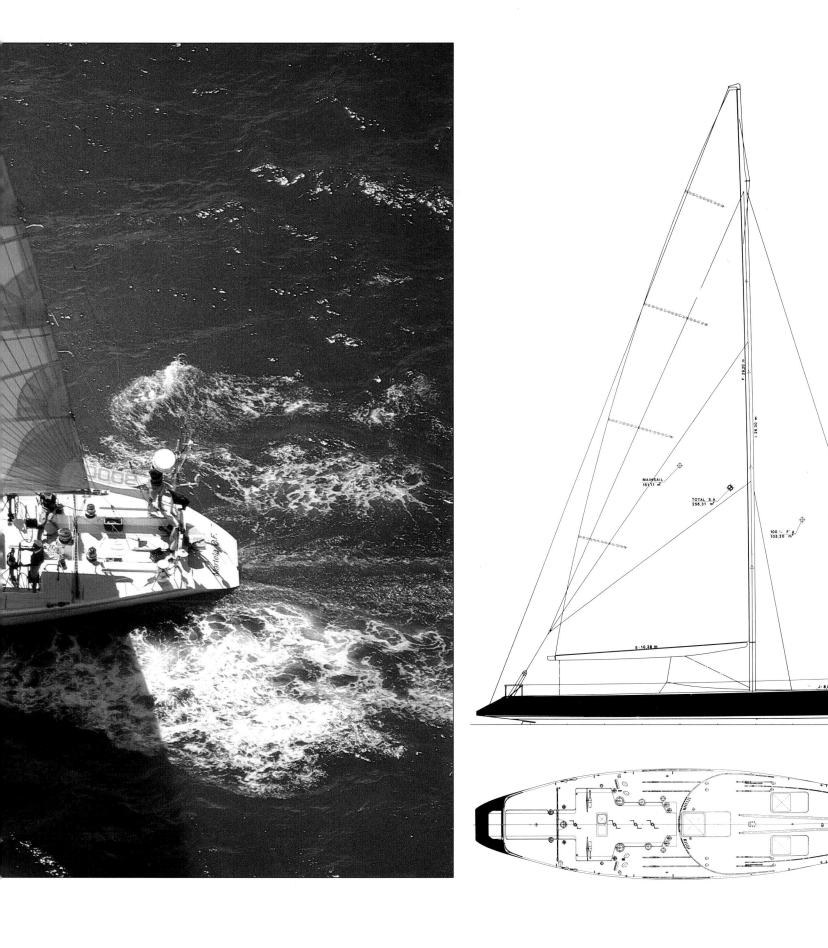

Martela O.F.

Merit

Skipper: Pierre Fehlmann

Personal: 48-years-old. Lives in Switzerland.

Professional Background: Degrees in engineering and business. Worked for IBM, and in the textile and chemical industries. Now involved in real estate and property development.

Sailing Background: Started sailing with mother "before I was born!" Sailed dinghies on Lake Geneva. Was Swiss champion on 505's five times, won the 505 European Championship in 1962. Finished second at the 1967 505 World Championship. Fourth on handicap in 1977/78 WTRTR on *Disque D'Or*; fourth on handicap in 1981/82 WTRTR on *Disque D'Or III*; first on elapsed time in 1985/86 WTRTW on *UBS Switzerland*. In 1988/89 won several races with *Merit* including Nioulargue, Discovery Race, Transat, and Lorient-St. Barts. Currently part-owner of *Belmont Finland II* (ex *UBS Switzerland*) and *Merit*. Has also owned *Gauloise*, and *Disque d'Or I, II, and III*.

Nautical Miles Logged: Approximately 200,000

Best Sailing Experience: Finishing second at the 505 World Championships in 1967.

Worst Experience: *Gauloise* breaking apart and sinking in a mid-Atlantic storm in 1976. "Rescued by a container ship...jumping on rescue nets at the side of the ship (in 1976) was at the limit!"

About *Merit*: Bruce Farr was asked to design the best possible boat for the Whitbread. After studies of weather patterns and tank testing, opted against the ketch rig. Peter Blake contributed as a consultant on sail trim and speed optimization.

About Crew: Carried 14 crew, most of whom had never sailed a maxi. Doctors changed at each leg, and an additional crew member came on board for the southern legs.

"I am not misanthropic, and I am not a slave driver, no matter what they say. I don't rant at my crew, but in events like the Whitbread Round the World Race, you cannot practice democracy."

Pierre Fehlmann

Merit

"You have to keep your troops motivated on long hauls where you don't see land or even ships for weeks on end. We're all in it together, but the responsibility for good teamwork lies with the captain."

Pierre Fehlmann

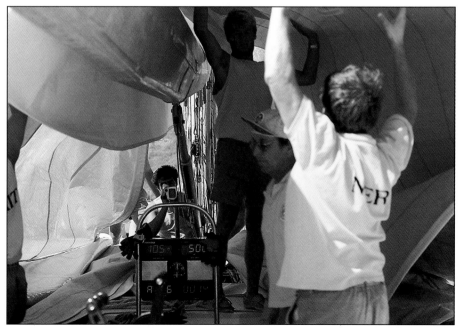

179

Merit

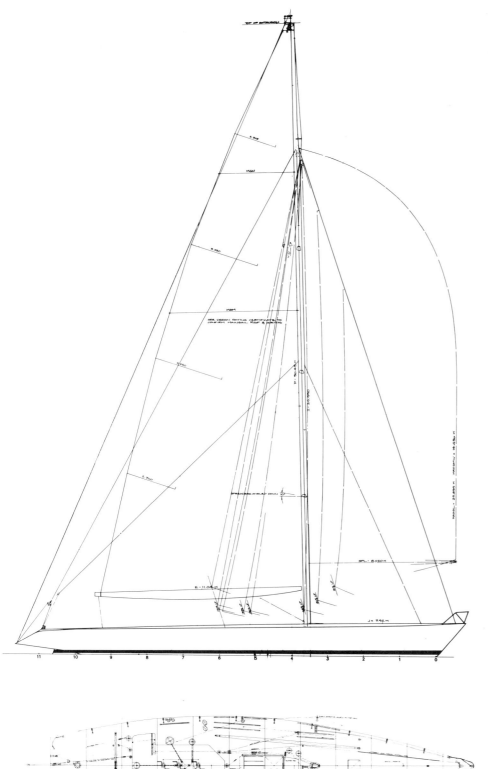

No other new generation of maxis has sailed and raced as many miles as Merit. Pierre Fehlmann devoted a tremendous amount of time and energy to planning a "winner." He did prove to have the fastest sloop, but as the race progressed, it turned out that the ketch rig was a better configuration for the WRTWR.

"The notion that sailboat people are more nautical than those who run power boats is pure nonsense. Anyone who buys either motor or sailboat must love the water, and how can you measure the intensity of someone's love?"

Pierre Fehlmann

Merit

"When the going gets rough, there is a kind of atavistic fear, native to all of us, that gets the adrenaline flowing and creates an inner excitement. Above all, there is the sheer joy of pitting oneself against the lethal forces of nature."

Pierre Fehlmann

Registry: Switzerland
Skipper: Pierre Fehlmann
Sail no. Z-3333
Captain: Gerald Rogivue/Dominique Wavre
Designer: Bruce Farr
Builder: Decision SA- Morges
Year: 1988
IOR-rating: 70'
LOA: 24.57m/ 80.61'
LWL: 19.68m/ 64.57
Beam: 5.45m/ 17.88'
Draft: 3.93m/ 12.89'
Displ: 32,649kg/ 71,978lbs.
Sail loft: North
Mainsail: 193m/ 2,078sq.ft.
Headsail: 160m/ 1,722sq.ft.
Spinnaker: 296m/ 3,186sq.ft.
Winches: Lewmar
Mast/rig type: Alusuisse and Favre/fractional
Construction material: FRP Composite
Construction method: Vacuum bagged
Engine: Volvo TAMD 31 A, 130HP
Generator: Volvo 2002 18HP
Electronics: 2 x DECKMAN PC
  Feedback Weather Satellite Receiver WSR524C
  Sony Solid State B/W Monitor
  NAGRAFAX - Nagra/Kudelski
  Furuno Radar model 1720
  GME 310 Satnav
  Navstar 603S Transit Satellite Navigator
  Magellan 1000 GPS Handheld Satellite Navigator
  Skanti SSB 400W TRP8400S
  SEA 322 HF/SSB 100W Radiotelephone
  INMARSAT Standard-C Telex SNEC
  Maritime Marine-Barograph
  VHF Husun 65
  B&G 390 Hercules System
  B&G 390 Hercules System Depthsounder
  B&G Course Indicator-Hadrian
  CRM 2651a Safety Watchkeeping Receiver
   2182 KHz
  TAIYO ADDF TDL 1520 Man Overboard
   Research
  3 x VHF ICOM IC-M11 Handheld

P. SCHILLER

Merit

NCB Ireland

Skipper: Joe English

Personal: 34-years-old. Wife April gave birth to their daughter Etha in January 1989, three hours after *NCB Ireland* left Dublin for St. Thomas. "I managed to get a motorboat to bring me back to shore!"

Professional Background: Studied business, but gave it up for a career as sailmaker. Started sailmaking in Ireland and in 1979 moved to Australia in connection with *Southern Cross*. Sailed extensively in Australia. Was involved in various campaigns, including the 1987 America's Cup (with South Australian Syndicate as sail coordinator and coach for the crew).

Sailing Background: Family has always sailed. Started in a dinghy and progressed up through various classes.

Subsequently raced on several yachts, with good results on board *Justine III* in 1981, which won the One Ton Cup and the same year on board *Hitchhiker*, winning the Two Ton Cup. Raced the Papua New Guinea Admiral's Cup: *Justine* in the 1985 and *Turkish Delight* in 1987.

Nautical Miles Logged: Never counted, but a rough estimate is 90,000 nautical miles.

About NCB Ireland:The weather predictions for the race indicated that only 10% of the race would be upwind with the majority of the race reaching and running. The design parameters were to be based on this prediction, but the project team requested that Ron Holland (the designer) add more stability for better upwind performance. "Our boat is a little heavier than the other boats since we also wanted to get stability. Our higher displacement gives us a better upwind performance than the others, but we are not as fast as the other yachts reaching and running." English adds that in retrospect, the extra stability was a mistake.

About Crew: "The crew is a balance between experienced sailors and newcomers to offshore racing. Three have done the race before on board *Atlantic Privateer* and *Drum*; we have a sailing master from *Condor*, a bowman from *KZ-1* and a naval officer. All together there are 16, counting seven Irish, six New Zealanders."

Future: After the Whitbread Race the plan is that *NCB Ireland* shall be used as a training yacht for youth and offshore sailors in Ireland, a program with which the English will be involved. "I also hope to be involved in a future Whitbread Race."

Registry: Ireland
Skipper: Joe English
Sail no. IR-1992
Designer: Ron Holland
Builder: Killian Bushe/Rob Lipsett
Year: 1988
IOR-rating: 70'
LOA: 24.25m/ 80.83'
LWL: 20.26m/ 66.42'
Beam: 6.09m/ 20'
Draft: 3.96m/ 13'
Displ: 31,564kg/ 69,440lbs.
Sail loft: North, Sobstad spinnaker
Mainsail: 199m/ 2,142sq.ft.
Headsail: 174m/ 1,873.sq.ft.
Spinnaker: 372m/ 4,004sq.ft.
Winches: Lewmar
Mast/rig type: Sparcraft/fractional
Construction material: Composite
Construction method: Vacuum bagged
Electronics: Furuno Weatherfax
  Furuno Satellite Navigator FSN-70
  Furuno GPS GP-300
  Furuno Radar Daylight Screen
  AP Navigator
  3M Storm Scope For Electric Activity WX10XA
  Feedback Weather Satellite Receiver WSR524C
  JVC Color Monitor
  Northstar 800X Loran-C
  B&G Hercules System 390
  B&G Hercules Depthsounder
  Digital Barograph
  Zenith 183 Compu Sail/Performance Program
  Compaq 286 - Comm. Weather-Digitalizer Board
  Skanti 250W SSB
  Skanti 400W SSB
  Skanti VHF 3000
  Shipcom Telex System

NCB Ireland

> *"Competing against the world's best racing yacht designers calls for an accurate and well-organized development program and an intuitive ability to assess the balance of design parameters which can win races under variable conditions."*
>
> Ron Holland

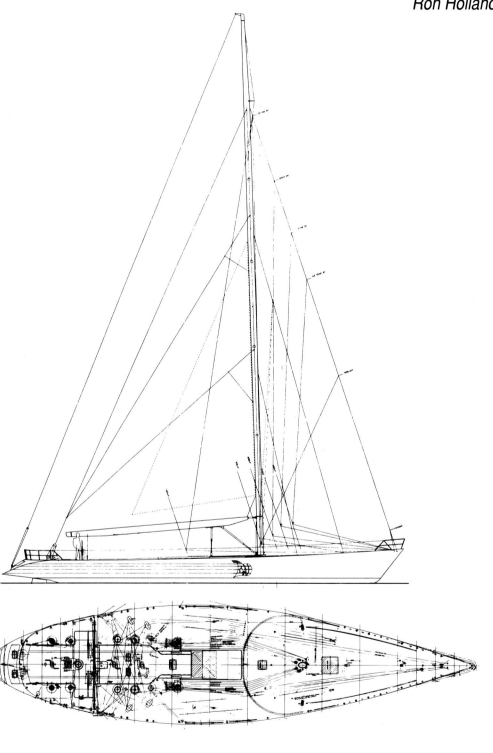

NCB Ireland

NCB Ireland, *one of the prettiest in the fleet, was Ireland's first entry in the Whitbread. She was named after her major sponsor, National and City Brokers of Dublin. Shortly before the start of the race, skipper Bob Campbell was replaced by Joe English.* NCB Ireland *had the rotten luck of breaking the boom three times, costing dearly in lost time.*

"The racing so far has been somewhat disappointing. On the first leg we were caught in the Doldrums; on the second leg we broke our boom, which we also did at the third leg. Across the Atlantic, from Newport to Cork, Fisher & Paykel beat us by over a day."

Joe English

NCB Ireland

Rothmans

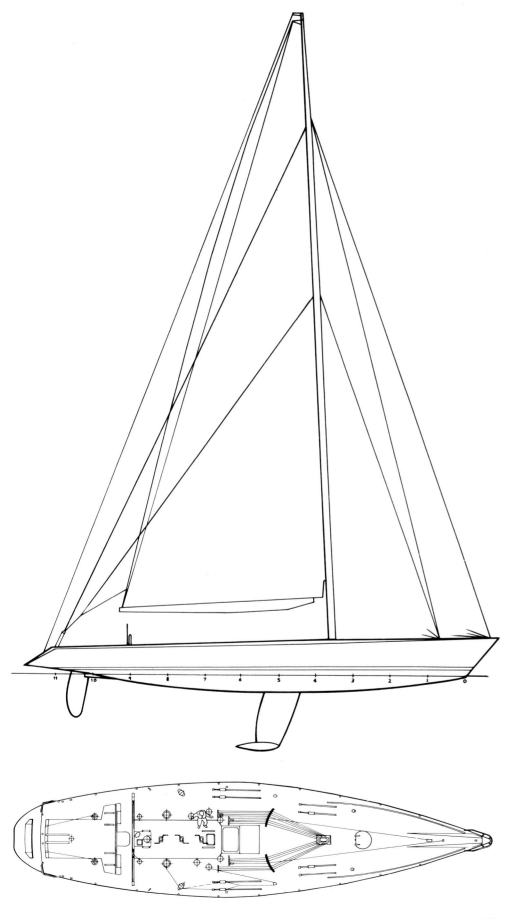

Registry: England
Skipper: Lawrie Smith
Sail no. K-100
Captain: Kym "Shag" Morton
Designer: Robert Humphreys
Builder: Paragon Composites Ltd.
Year: 1989
IOR-rating: 70'
LOA: 24.54m/ 81'
LWL: 20.14m/ 66'
Beam: 5.98m/ 19.62'
Draft: 3.82m/ 12.53'
Displ: 29,000kg/ 63,933lbs.
Sail loft: North
Mainsail: 179.2m/ 1,930sq.ft.
Headsail: 161m/ 1,733sq.ft.
Spinnaker: 356.4m/ 3,836sq.ft.
Winches: Lewmar
Mast/rig type: Sparcraft/fractional
Construction material: Composite
Construction method: Vacuum bagged
Electronics: Furuno DFAX
  Magnavox MX4102 Satellite Navigator
  Trimble Navigation Loran-GPS 10X Navigator
  Furuno Radar Daylight Screen
  AP Navigator
  SP 2182 KHz Watchkeeping Receiver
    Type R501
  Feedback Weather Satellite Receiver
    WSR524C
  Sony Color Monitor
  Navstar 2000 Satellite Navigator
  B&G Hercules System 390
  B&G Hercules Depthsounder 390
  Digital Barograph/Aneroid Barometer Mark 2
  Nagrafax
  Dary Com
  Express Writer 301 Toshiba A8760U Type II
  Toshiba PC
  ICOM IC-M700UK
  RM Nimbus Color Monitor
  Skanti 400W HF-SSB Radio System,
    Type TRP400S
  ICOM VHF IC-M100
  Shipcom 600 Radio Telex System
  Summa Sketch Plus - Summagraphics
  Deckman Computer
  Connections Computer Multiport Data Switch
    - Telex/tablet

Rothmans

Skipper: Lawrie Smith

Personal: 33-years-old. From Titchfield, Hampshire, U.K.

Professional Background: Sailor. Sold dinghy equipment and spars for five years to support sailing.

Sailing Background: Born into sailing family. Started sailing dinghies at age six. Has won several dinghy championships in England and worldwide. Also made a name for himself in multihulls, IOR and transoceanic racing. Participated in three America's Cup campaigns: skippered *Lionheart* and *Victory*, and acted as advisor to *Kookaburra*.

Nautical Miles Logged: No idea.

Best Sailing Experience: The America's Cup in 1983.

Worst Experience: The Olympic boycott in 1980, after having trained for three years.

About *Rothmans*: Unusual project; Rothmans decided to do the Whitbread, and approached the designer, Rob Humphreys. He in turn chose the builder, Adrian Thompson. They approached Smith afterwards. They examined the ketch rig, but decided against it.

About Crew: 14 crew members — "I think it's the good guys who come from dinghies..."

Future: Probably join Peter DeSavary in his next America's Cup campaign.

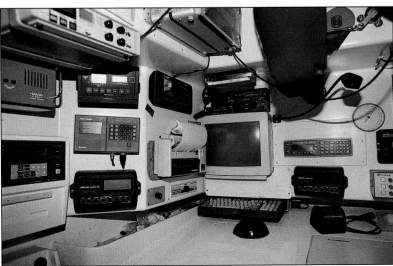

Rothmans *has perhaps the most professional international crew of all the maxis. While money can buy some advantage, the bottom line for successful round the world racing is good seamanship, tactical awareness and slick boat handling!*

Rothmans

Satquote British Defender

Skipper: Colin Watkins

Personal: 40-years-old. Married, with two sons. Commander in the Royal Navy.

Sailing Background: Started sailing in dinghies at age 11. Raced Dragons. First raced offshore as bowman in 1966. Mostly has raced as navigator/tactician. Skippered first big yacht in 1969. Raced two transatlantics. Sailed first Whitbread on *Adventure*. Joined *Satquote Brittish Defender* project full-time in March 1989.

Nautical Miles Logged: Estimates 70,000-80,000

Most Impressive Sailing Experience: The second leg of the last Whitbread, "...unbelievable experience, to be going so fast downwind...I think the most scary was when I needed to convince the crew that it was quite safe, which it wasn't really of course, to be running downwind in thick fog very fast — 28-29 knots — you could just see the forestay. I knew there were icebergs around us...the radar was on now and again; we suddenly saw a blip one-and-a-half miles away, and the blip then moved cross to the middle and then to the left but never got any closer...and I just called up for any yacht in our position on the VHF...and it was *NCB Ireland* crossing our bow on the opposite jibe...we never saw each other at all!"

About *Satquote British Defender*: Boat was designed for the Whitbread as a project directed by Chris Freer for Sports Sponsorship International. Martin Francis was design leader. Worked with data on Whitbread as it is today. According to Frank Esson (former skipper), the Navy was looking for a sponsor for the Whitbread. The owner at the time was building a boat for the race, and wanted the Navy to manage the project. "Through a complex series of negotiations the Navy handed over the challenge to the Army, and the Army realized early on that it was such a big undertaking to sail a state-of-the-art maxi in the Whitbread that it should be a combined services event."

About Crew: 15 crew: two civilians and 13 servicemen. It was initially decided to have three crews, which would change as the race progressed. After the first transatlantic race, followed by the Lorient-St. Barts race against *Merit* and *Baltic* Maxi, it became obvious that the whole plan, although on schedule, was made too complex — so it was back to one primary crew with just a few members changing, like the doctor."

Watkins started as navigator, and when three-crew concept was changed to single crew, he was named skipper. In last race he was skipper/navigator/watch leader which he feels didn't work well as there was too much to do for it to work properly.

Future: Boat goes back to owner after race. "I think I'll go back to day racing for a while."

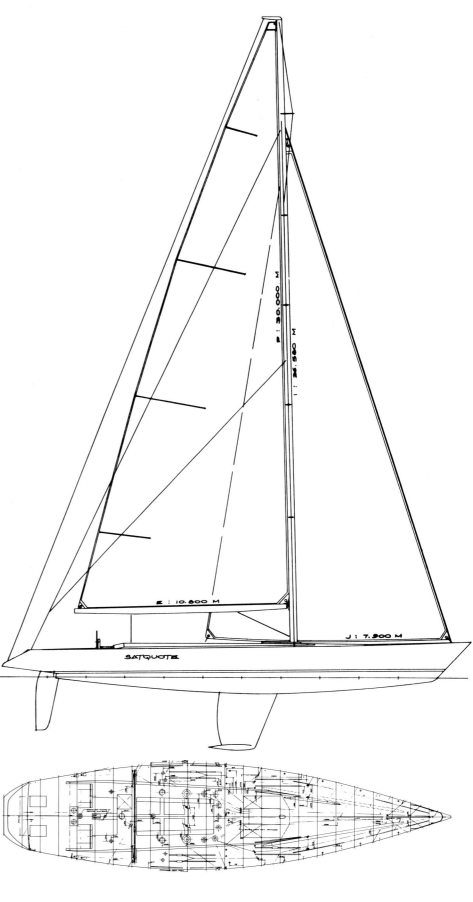

P: 30.000 M

I: 26.580 M

E: 10.800 M

J: 7.900 M

SATQUOTE

Satquote British Defender

Registry: England
Owner: Klaus Hebben
Skipper: Commander Colin Watkins
Sail no. K 303
Designer: Martin Francis/Jacques Fauroux
Captain: Serge Guilhaumou
Builder: Green Marine
Year: 1989
IOR-rating: 69.99'
LOA: 24.2m/ 79.42'
LWL: 21.03m/ 69'
Beam: 5.75m/ 18.83'
Draft: 3.81m/ 12.5'
Displ: 30,545kg/ 67,339lbs.
Sail loft: Sobstad/Hood
Mainsail: 127.4m/ 1,371sq.ft.
Headsail: 154.13m/ 1,659sq.ft.
Spinnaker: 210m/ 2,260sq.ft.
Winches: Lewmar
Mast/rig type: Proctor/fractional
Construction material: Composite
Construction method: Vacuum bagged
Engine: Volvo Penta
Generator: HFL
Electronics: Mitsubishi Monitor
  Feedback Weather Satellite Receiver WSR524C
  Simrad Taiyo ADDF TD-L 1520/
    Man overboard locator
  Furuno DFAX
  Shipmate RS 5100 Satellite Navigator
  Shipmate RS 4000 CC Radio Navigation System
  S.P Watchkeeping Receiver
  Furuno Radar GaAs Fet Front End.
    4-tone Daylight display
  Skanti 400W Receiver/Transmitter TRP0400
  B&G Hydra 330
  B&G Hercules System 390
  Navstar 2000 Satellite Navigator
  ICOM VHF IC-M55
  Toshiba 5100
  Toshiba Express Writer 301
  Rigil Digital Barograph
  Deckman Computer

The potential for being highly competitive was there. Satquote British Defender *proved she was definitely capable of a lot of speed as she kept right up with the top four boats. Nonetheless, the combined forces of Navy and Army did not have time to gain the racing experience that the crew members of the other leading boats had.*

Satquote British Defender

Steinlager 2

Skipper: Peter Blake

Personal: "40, feeling 90." Born and raised in Auckland, New Zealand. He and British wife Pippa—also an avid sailor—have two children. (When the oldest was two, she went along on 14,000-mile delivery trip from New Zealand to Britain on *Lion New Zealand*.)

Professional Background: Professional yachtsman, not only in generally accepted sense, but including public relations and promotional aspects of a project like *Steinlager 2*. Main income derives from TV commercials.

Sailing Background: "I have always been sailing. Before I could walk, my family took me out sailing in dinghies. Whenever we went on an outing it was always by sailing." Sailed all previous Whitbread races; won the Sidney-Hobart race twice at line honors, once on handicap. Was on board *Condor* when she took line honors and set a new record for the Fastnet in 1979.

Nautical Miles Logged: Estimated 375,000

Best Sailing Experience: "There are so many I could call my best experience. Of course, the more you do this, the more it takes to give you a thrill."

Worst Experience: "Most likely the 1984 Sidney-Hobart Race, even though we finished first on *Lion New Zealand*. It was like another Fastnet Race. It was a horrible time, a shocking time, although only one life was lost compared to the Fastnet Race disaster in 1979."

About *Steinlager 2*: Designed specifically for the Whitbread Race. When Bruce Farr was contacted he already had commissions for three other one-off maxi yachts and one general commission. Security was therefore crucial, as it was quite important that the information given him would not be incorporated in anyone else's boat, and vice versa. "It was our idea to have a ketch, and when we asked for a fractional rig, Bruce [Farr] was not at all keen to run the test... My father has had a fractional ketch for the last 30 years, and when she competes against her sister ship, a masthead-rigged ketch, she always beats her with big margin. It just seems that the sail combination is more suitable. We are extremely happy with the result.

"The first hull that was built, there was something wrong with one of the resins. It delaminated. The builders themselves questioned the resin at the time. The delamination had absolutely nothing to do with overbaking, aluminum space frames... all the conjecture about it is ridiculous." When the second hull for *Steinlager 2* was built, all materials were verified from SP Systems, with terrific results.

About Crew: Seven of the crew (including Blake) were on board *Lion New Zealand*, and two sailed the last Whitbread on *NZI Enterprise*. The rest have considerable experience racing in the Admiral's Cup or America's Cup, as well as sailing dinghies for the New Zealand National Team.

Future: "When the Whitbread is over, I plan a long vacation with my family. After that, I cannot tell. I would like to stick with the same sponsor. A lot depends on how successful *Steinlager 2* is." Also has plans to write a book about the Whitbread.

Steinlager 2

Registry: New Zealand
Skipper: Peter Blake, MBE
Sail no. KZ-2
Captain: Brad Butterworth
Designer: Bruce Farr
Builder: Southern Pacific Boatyard, Ltd.
Year: 1989
IOR-rating: 70.05'
LOA: 25.49m/ 83.63'
LWL: 20.29m/ 66.57'
Beam: 5.76m/ 18.9'
Draft: 3.99m/ 13.09'
Displ: 35,177kg/ 77,551lbs.
Sail loft: North
Mainsail: 163m/ 1,754.6sq.ft.
Headsail: 158m/ 1,701sq.ft.
Spinnaker: 291m/ 3,132sq.ft.
Mizzen: 81m/ 872sq.ft.
Mizzen staysail: 196m/ 2,110sq.ft.
Winches: Lewmar
Mast/rig type: Fractional Ketch
Construction material: FRP Composite
Construction method: Vacuum bagged
Electronics: Furuno DFAX
  Magnavox MX4102 Satellite Navigator
  Trimble Navigation Loran-GPS 10X
  SP 2182 KHz Watchkeeping Receiver Type R501
  Feedback Weather Satellite Receiver WSR524C
  B&G Hercules System 390
  B&G Hercules Depthsounder 390
  SP Receiver Type R1119
  SP Exciter Type S1303
  SP Transmitter Type T1135
  SP VHF C403/Remote Control Unit H410
  Thrane & Thrane TT-3210A Radio Telex Modem
  Pakratt 232 Modem Switch for Still Photo
  Mitsubishi Video Copy Processor
  Groupmen CTV/Monitor-Satellite Weather Picture
  Citizen Satellite Navigation Timing System
  Apple Macintosch SE - Keyboard & Mouse
  Meteostar 2000 Microprocessor Controlled Baroscope

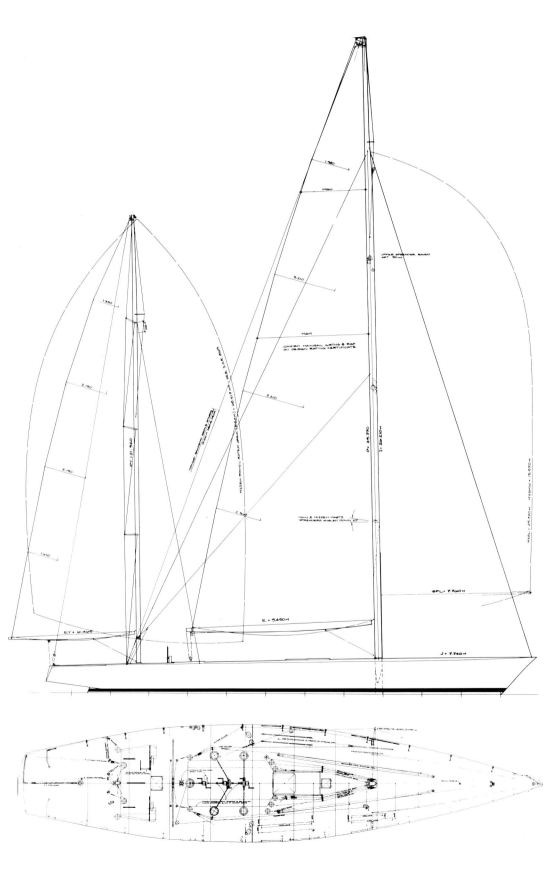

Steinlager 2

"You don't have to have your boat full of water for the Fastnet but you sure do for the start of the Whitbread... What sort of food do you have on board, do the guys get on well, are you going to have a big fight after four days. There are so many more factors apart from the speed aspect: durability, how good your rigging is, how good are your fittings, are you paying enough attention to the overall planning and preparation. If you haven't done that you can have the fastest boat in the world and you won't win."

Peter Blake

Steinlager 2

The Card

Registry: Sweden
Skipper: Roger Nilson
Co-skipper: Magnus Olsson
Sail no. 42624
Designer: Bruce Farr
Builder: Eric Goetz, USA
Year: 1988
IOR-rating: 70'
LOA: 24.03m/ 78.84'
LWL: 19.32m/ 63.39'
Beam: 5.63m/ 18.47'
Draft: 4.13m/ 13.55'
Displ: 30,012kg/ 66,164lbs.
Sail loft: North
Mainsail: 123m/ 1,324sq.ft.
Headsail: 174m/ 1,873sq.ft.
Spinnaker: 321m/ 3,455sq.ft.
Mizzen: 70m/ 754sq.ft.
Mizzen staysail: 170m/ 1,830sq.ft.
Winches: Lewmar
Mast/rig type: Masthead Ketch
Construction material: FRP Composite
Construction method: Vacuum bagged
Electronics: Furuno DFAX
  Shipmate RS5100 Satellite Navigator
  Trimble Navigation Loran-GPS 10X
  Furuno Radar GaAs Daylight Screen
  AP Navigator
  SP 2182 KHz Watchkeeping Receiver Type R501
  B&G Hercules System 390
  B&G Hercules Depthsounder 390
  Skanti 400W HF-SSB Radio System, Type TRP8403S
  ICOM VHF IC-M100
  Sea 222 Synthesized SSB Radiotelephone
  Micro Scribe Computer 440P11
  Digital Computer
  I&M Macsea Station Informatique De Navigation

The Card

Skipper: Roger Nilson

Personal: 40-years-old. From Sweden.

Professional Background: Trained as doctor. Worked for two years in a surgery clinic in Stockholm. Has almost completed orthopedic surgeon qualification. Recently more involved in sailing. Produced a documentary on sailing for Swedish TV.

Sailing Background: Started sailing at age nine, racing at 21. Originally raced Star boats and Solings; has owned a J-24.
Since then skippered four or five boats in offshore racing.
Raced since 1971, mostly as navigator — sailing Admiral's Cups, Sardinia Cups, SORC, one-ton worlds, as well as racing on 12-meters and 6-meters. Has had limited experience skippering large boats. Currently a professional sailor, living aboard *The Card*. Has only been actively sailing her for the last year. Spent previous 20 months promoting the project and looking for sponsors.

Nautical Miles Logged: Approximately 120,000

Best Sailing Experience: Racing a 75' catamaran in the Round-Europe Race.

Worst Experience: Losing the keel on *Drum* in the 1985 Fastnet.

About *The Card*: Skip Novak and John Baker did a computer analysis and determined that a ketch would be faster than a sloop on this course. When Nilson took over the boat in April 1988, there was no reason to change.

About Crew: "Many of the crew do not need much skippering; they know what to do. It's more soft leadership."

Future: Has contract to write another book. Maybe start another sailing project. "Of course you gain a lot of experience about the business side of these projects. I have been managing this project even though I am sailing the boat. All the commercial rights are owned by a company that I own."

The Card

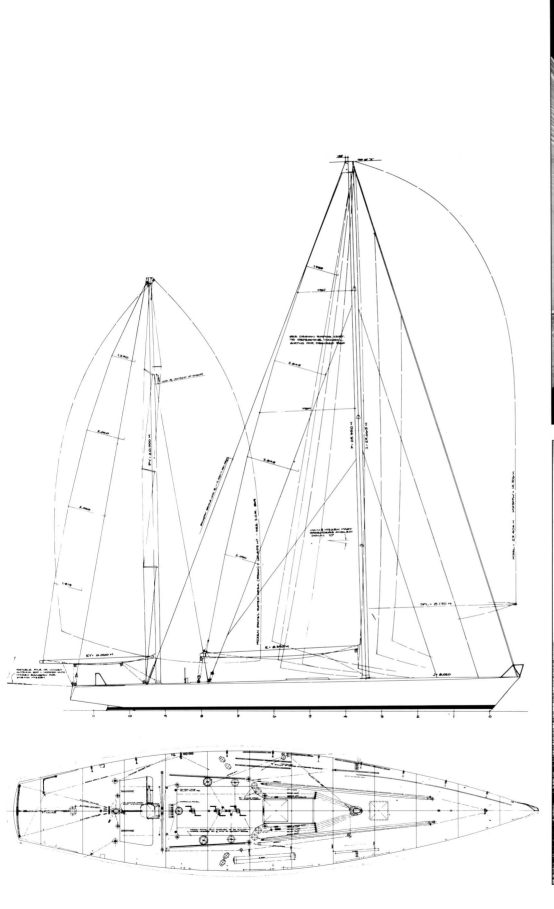

The Card

Losing the mizzen mast just eight minutes after the start in Auckland, New Zealand. The rig caught a spectator boat, which almost capsized, but The Card's rig came down instead.

214

Roger Nilson, Magnus Olsson and the rest of the crew worked extremely hard to keep this project charging ahead. The tragic death of Janne Gustavson in a motorbike accident after the first leg in Punta del Este, Uruguay, was a big blow to crew morale. Nonetheless, optimism and perseverance enabled them to regain their position.

Editor's Note: The Card *was purchased by Ted Turner, Jr. in Spring, 1990.*

The Card

Union Bank of Finland

Registry: Finland
Skipper: Ludde Ingvall
Co-skipper: Lars Fellman
Sail no. L 8008
Designer: Joubert-Nivelt
Builder: Laivateollisuus OY
Year: 1988
IOR-rating: 70'
LOA: 25.2m/ 82.67'
LWL: 20.9m/ 68.58'
Beam: 5.8m/ 19.03'
Draft: 3.9m/ 12.75'
Displ: 29,222kg/ 64,288lbs.
Ballast: 13,500kg/ 29,762lbs.
Sail loft: North
Mainsail: 205m/ 2,207sq.ft.
Headsail: 165m/ 1,776sq.ft.
Spinnaker: 365m/ 3,929sq.ft.
Winches: Lewmar
Mast/rig type: Nokia Aluminum/fractional
Constr. material: Deck Composite with Nomex core
   Hull Aluminum alloy ALMg 4.5 Mn
Constr. method: Welded and vacuum bagged
Engine: MTU 100 HP diesel
Generator: Dynawatt
Electronics: Furuno Weather Fax DFAX 280 A/N
   Furuno FSN-90 Satellite Navigator-Trasit
   Furuno GPS GP-300 Navstar System
   Furuno Color Radar 36 SM • Furuno Loran
   Furuno VHF FM-2510 • Furuno VHF FM-55 Handhold
   Furuno SSB FS-4001 • Furuno AD Converter AD-10S
   AP Navigator
   Skanti Watch Receiver WR 6000
   B&G Hercules System 390
   B&G Hercules Depthsounder 390
   Suunto Flushgate Compass Repeater
   Aneres Barograph VM Electronic
   Inmarsat Standard A-Comsat Telesystems MCS-9100
   Feedback Weather Satellite Receiver WSR524C
   Vanguard Satellite Receiver FMR-260-PL
   Trommel Sextant Carl Zeiss
   Canon PC
   Apple Macintosh II CX PC • Apple Image Writer II
   Apple Fax Modem
   Digital Board Hurta IS/ADB
   Pakratt 232 Modem for Computer
   Sony ICF 2001D All Band Radio Receiver
   2 x Sony Super Fine Pitch Color Monitor RGB-VGA
   Nokia Modem DS61101/VB312
   Airphone MP-3S to deck
   Sailmath Deckman Computer
   Seafix 2000 Seafarer Range RDP
   Software: Mac Sea to Apple PC
   Satellite Data System
   Morse and Telex Decoding
   Storage of Satellite Picture for Still Photos

Union Bank of Finland *has the most advanced communications systems of any of the boats. (Luckily, she was at hand when* Martela O.F. *sent her MAYDAY in February, 1990.)*

Many new items were invented to save weight, and a whole new concept for the below deck lay-out enabled the off-watch crew to enjoy more peace and rest. After arriving in Auckland under jury rig, Ludde Ingval joked that UBF stands for "Usually Breaks First." He also said, "We are not the last maxi but the fourth ketch."

Skipper: Ludde Ingval

Personal: 34-years-old. Born in Helsinki. Married during 1985/86 Whitbread race, has two daughters.

Professional Background: Graduated from university in l974. Joined Navy. Started several small businesses which were later sold. Enjoys managing projects.

Sailing Background: Grew up sailing. Father raced Dragons. Started in dinghies, then 505's. Skied winters and sailed summers. Finally left Finland for places "where there was sun and open seas all the time."

Nautical Miles Logged: About 150,000. "You know, you stop counting. Sailing has been my life. I have spent more time in a boat than I have in a car."

Best Sailing Experience: Winning the second leg of the Whitbread Race in 1985/86 after being dismasted on the first leg. Built a new mast in Cape Town and then beat *NZ Enterprise* to New Zealand by 7 1/2 minutes.

Worst Experience: On *Atlantic Privateer* when the mast came down. "It was ironic, we had been discussing the fact that the boat would break up if we kept up that speed."

About *Union Bank of Finland*: Started with clean slate. We were first to get sponsor money, and so had the time to try different ideas. "The first design brief was to take white paper and try the craziest ideas that came to mind. We threw away some really interesting crazy ideas and we threw away a hell of a lot of absolutely dumb crazy ideas, and we were left with a few options. The most aggressive option of the ones that we thought were reasonable, which would have a chance to succeed, was the one that was showing the most promise...I would say that our boat is a different concept from everybody else's. You look at it, it looks different."

"We did extensive tank testing, over a thousand pulls, as well as wind tunnel tests of the bottom of the boat. Also considerable work on keel profile, and the joint between keel and hull.

"They [the designers] have produced a boat that is better than the boat that I ordered. If we don't win, it's not because of them. We're happy and I just hope that the crew and I can do the boat justice."

About Crew: All Finnish. Seven or eight have sailed the Whitbread before. Eight are Olympic sailors. All have high technical skills, and participated in the building of the boat as well as designing the various systems — for example, the navigator designed electronic system. The team has sailed about 30,000 miles together.

Future: "In 10 months' time *Union Bank of Finland* will be for sale. A winning boat is easy to sell. Maybe I will be for sale, too!"

"Write a book? Maybe for my children, so they can have a record of how nuts their father's been."

KANSA MERCEDES-BENZ NOKIA ALUMINIUM SALLY ALBATROSS RUKKA SONY MATKA-KALEVA UNIMED LTD CANON WÄRTSILÄ

UNION BANK OF FINLAND

UNION BANK OF FINLAND

Arriving under jury rig in Auckland, New Zealand after sailing more than 300 nautical miles as the "fourth ketch."

"I think that when you are doing this kind of thing you have two lives. The life aboard a maxi yacht is something you cannot describe. When you step off the boat , have a shower, sleep in a comfortable bed, watch TV, have a nice dinner... your life at sea is unrealistic. Similarly, when you are on the boat, until you step ashore, life ashore seems from a different planet. And on these two planets I have had such different experiences that have been good."

Ludde Ingval

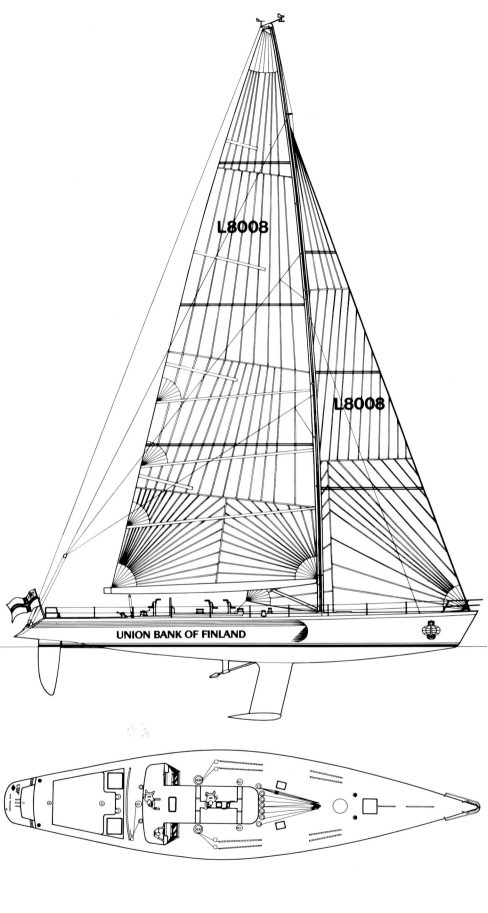

Union Bank of Finland

Whitbread Round the World Race Results

**RESULTS FROM THE FIVE WHITBREAD ROUND THE WORLD RACES ONLY INCLUDE YACHTS ABOVE IOR RATING OF 60 FEET.
TIMES ARE GIVEN AS ELAPSED TIME AS WELL AS RESULTS.**

WHITBREAD ROUND THE WORLD RACE 1973/74

The following boats in class A:
IOR 68.0' Ketch Burton Cutter, Leslie Williams and Alan Smith, England
IOR 69.0' Ketch Great Britain II, Chay Blyth, England
IOR 63.5' Ketch Pen Duick VI, Eric Tabarly, France

1. Leg Portsmouth, England - Cape Town, South Africa, 6,650 miles
DD HH MM SS
42 00 17 40 Burton Cutter
43 04 52 10 Great Britain II
55 02 14 10 Pen Duick VI, broke the mast. Sailed to Rio de Janeiro where
a new mast was stepped.

2. Leg Cape Town - Sydney, Australia, 6,600 miles
29 08 25 43 Pen Duick VI
29 17 16 46 Great Britain II
Burton Cutter returned to Port Elizabeth, South Africa due to a leak on
starboard side. Caught up with the race in Rio de Janeiro.

3. Leg Sydney - Rio de Janeiro, Brazil, 8,370 miles
40 16 03 58 Great Britain II
Penduick VI broke her mast again. Returned to Sydney and quit the race.

4. Leg Rio de Janeiro - Portsmouth, 5,500 miles
30 20 30 51 Great Britain II
32 23 36 51 Burton Cutter

Winner on elapsed time 27,120 miles
144 10 43 44 Great Britain II
Winner on handicap: Ketch Sayula II, Ramon Carlin, Mexico

WHITBREAD ROUND THE WORLD RACE 1977/78

The following boats in class A:
IOR 69.0' Ketch Great Britain II, Robert James, England
IOR 68.8' M-Sloop Heath's Condor, Leslie Williams legs 1 + 3 and Robin
Knox-Johnston legs 2 + 4, England
Ketch Pen Duick VI, Eric Tabarly, France

1. Leg Portsmouth, England - Cape Town, South Africa, 6,650 miles
DD HH MM SS
40 05 36 00 Great Britain II
50 07 28 48 Heath's Condor, broke the mast. Sailed to Monrovia and
stepped a new aluminum mast instead of the penalized glass fiber mast.

2. Leg Cape Town - Auckland, New Zealand, 7,400 miles
33 16 46 12 Great Britain II
33 17 10 12 Heath's Condor

3. Leg Auckland - Rio de Janeiro, Brazil, 7.400 miles
30 09 03 36 Heath's Condor
31 06 34 12 Great Britain II
Pen Duick VI was the first to cross the finishing line in Rio, but she did not
have a valid racing certificate since she had a spent uranium keel.
The IOR had changed the rule in 1975 to disallow any material for keels
with higher specific gravity than lead.

4. Leg Rio de Janeiro - Portsmouth, 5,500 miles
28 15 59 24 Heath's Condor
29 07 25 48 Great Britain II

Winner on elapsed time 26,950 miles
134 12 22 47 Great Britain II
143 01 41 59 Heath's Condor
Winner on handicap: Ketch, Flyer, Cornelis van Rietschoten, Holland

WHITBREAD ROUND THE WORLD RACE 1981/82

The following boats in class A:
IOR 62.9' F-Sloop Ceramco New Zealand, Peter Blake, New Zealand
IOR 60.8' Ketch Euromarche*, Eric Tabarly, France
IOR 68.5' M-Sloop First Co-Operative, Leslie Williams, England
IOR 67.9' M-Sloop Flyer, Cornelis van Rietschoten, Holland
IOR 68.0' M-Sloop United Friendly**, Chay Blyth, England
* ex-Pen Duick VI ** ex-Great Britain II

1. Leg Portsmouth, England - Cape Town, South Africa, 7,010 miles
DD HH MM SS
36 10 56 37 Flyer
39 18 15 32 First Co-Operative
42 02 40 30 Euromarche
44 22 46 07 United Friendly
47 07 28 05 Ceramco New Zealand broke the mast. Continued under
jury rig.

2. Leg Cape Town - Auckland, New Zealand, 7,101 miles
30 04 27 30 Flyer
30 12 51 14 Ceramco New Zealand
32 04 45 47 Euromarche
33 18 15 32 First Co-Operative
35 20 03 14 United Friendly

3. Leg Auckland - Mara del Plata, Argentina, 6.030 miles
24 01 22 20 Flyer
24 08 39 24 Ceramco New Zealand
25 09 24 50 Euromarche
27 04 37 03 First Co-Operative
27 19 45 51 United Friendly

4. Leg Mara del Plata - Portsmouth, 6,149 miles
29 13 47 47 Flyer
30 06 56 55 Ceramco New Zealand
34 22 37 35 Euromarche
35 07 48 38 United Friendly
38 07 46 02 First Co-Operative broke the mast. Continued under jury rig.

Winner on elapsed time 26,647 miles and position in the 29 strong fleet:
120 06 34 14 Flyer
132 11 55 38 Ceramco New Zealand (3)
134 15 24 42 Euromarche (5)
138 15 27 12 First Co-Operative (6)
143 13 00 28 United Friendly (9)
Winner on handicap as well: Flyer

WHITBREAD ROUND THE WORLD RACE 1985/86

The following boats in class A:
IOR 69,0' M-Sloop Atlantic Privateer*, Peter "Padda" Kuttel, USA
IOR 69.6' M-Sloop Cote d'Or, Eric Tabarly, Belgium
IOR 69.3' M-Sloop Drum, Skip Novak, England
IOR 68.6' M-Sloop Lion New Zealand, Peter Blake, New Zealand
IOR 67.1' M-Sloop Norsk Data GB**, Bob Salmon, England
IOR 70.0' F-Sloop NZI Enterprise, Digby Taylor, New Zealand
IOR 69.4' F-Sloop UBS Switzerland, Pierre Fehlmann
* Sailed 1. leg as Portatan ** ex-Great Britain II

1. Leg Portsmouth, England - Cape Town, South Africa, 7,010 miles
DD HH MM SS
34 01 39 20 UBS Switzerland
34 17 46 47 Lion New Zealand
34 23 28 26 Cote d'Or, problem with delaminating.
35 09 06 42 NZI Enterprise
36 16 44 23 Drum (7), problem with delaminating.
39 15 09 53 Norsk Data GB (10)
Atlantic Privateer retired. Mast broken.

2. Leg Cape Town - Auckland, New Zealand, 7,101 miles
29 03 09 36 Atlantic Privateer
29 03 11 56 NZI Enterprise
29 04 59 22 UBS Switzerland
29 13 31 04 Drum
29 18 58 12 Lion New Zealand
30 20 07 06 Cote d'Or
35 00 02 49 Norsk Data GB (12)

3. Leg Auckland - Punta del Este, Uruguay, 6.255 miles
24 14 11 20 UBS Switzerland
24 23 30 35 Drum
25 00 50 25 Atlantic Privateer
25 01 09 11 Cote d'Or
25 22 53 59 Lion New Zealand
27 15 45 41 Norsk Data GB (9)
NZI Enterprise, broke the mast and retired.

4. Leg Punta del Este - Portsmouth, 6,281 miles
29 17 41 40 UBS Switzerland
31 09 46 12 Cote d'Or
31 13 08 29 Drum
31 18 52 00 Lion New Zealand
32 01 55 49 Atlantic Privateer
34 18 17 13 Norsk Data GB (9)

Winner on elapsed time 26,647 miles
117 14 31 42 UBS Switzerland
122 06 31 58 Lion New Zealand
122 18 54 31 Drum
126 08 27 33 Cote d'Or
138 01 15 36 Norsk Data GB (9)
Winner on handicap: L'Esprit d'Equipe, Lionel Pean, France

WHITBREAD ROUND THE WORLD RACE 1989/90

The following boats in Class A.
IOR 70.00' F-Sloop Belmont Finland II*, Harry Harkimo, Finland IOR 70.00'
F-Sloop Charles Jourdan, Alain Gabby, France
IOR 70.00' F-Sloop Fazisi, Skip Novak, USSR
IOR 70.00' M-Ketch Fisher & Paykel, Grant Dalton, New Zealand
IOR 70.00' F-Sloop Fortuna Extra Lights, Jan Santana, Spain
IOR 70.00' F-Sloop Gatorade, Giorgio Falck, Italy
IOR 70.00' M-Sloop Liverpool Enterprise, Bob Salmon, England
IOR 70.00' F-Sloop Martela O.F., Markku Wiikeri, Finland
IOR 70.00' F-Sloop Merit, Pierre Fehlmann, Switzerland
IOR 70.00' F-Sloop NCB Ireland, Bob English, Ireland
IOR 70.00' F-Sloop Rothmans, Lawrie Smith, England
IOR 70.00' F-Sloop Satquote British Defender, Colin Watkins, England
IOR 70.00' F-Ketch Steinlager II, Peter Blake, New Zealand
IOR 70.00' M-Ketch The Card, Roger Nilson, Sweden
IOR 70.00' F-Sloop Union Bank of Finland, Ludde Ingvall, Finland

1. Leg Southampton, England - Punta del Este, Uruguay, 6.280 miles
DD HH MM SS
25 20 46 27 Steinlager 2
26 08 11 20 Merit
27 03 50 26 Fisher & Paykel
27 07 29 00 Rothmans
28 06 43 25 The Card
28 13 20 18 Fazisi
28 13 22 58 Gatorade
28 13 54 58 Martela O.F.
28 14 23 52 Satquote British Defender
28 19 49 45 Fortuna Extra Lights
28 20 10 18 Charles Jourdan
28 20 21 15 Belmont Finland II
29 05 27 46 NCB Ireland
29 13 49 05 Union Bank of Finland
32 03 15-55 Liverpool Enterprise

2. Leg Punta del Este - Fremantle, Australian, 7.500 miles
Combined leg 1 + 2
27 05 34 44 Steinlager 2, 1
27 07 07 28 Rothmans, 4
27 07 07 56 Merit, 2
27 08 30 20 Fisher & Paykel, 3
27 22 16 41 Charles Jourdan, 7
27 22 57 57 The Card, 5
28 01 27 57 Martela O.F., 6
28 05 13 52 Union Bank of Finland, 11
28 05 52 22 Fortuna Extra Lights, 8
29 01 40 15 Fazisi, 9
29 05 39 14 Gatorade *, 10
29 10 01 43 Satquote British Defender, 12
29 10 39 02 NCB Ireland, 14
29 15 57 55 Belmont Finland II, 13
33 03 00 26 Liverpool Enterprise, 15
*Elapsed time modified by international jury

3. Leg Fremantle - Auckland, New Zealand, 3.480 miles
Combined leg 1 + 2 + 3
12 17 33 00 Steinlager 2, 1
12 17 39 04 Fisher & Paykel, 3
12 18 44 17 Merit, 2
12 18 54 37 Rothmans, 4
12 20 49 50 The Card, 5
12 21 22 22 Fortuna Extra Lights, 8
12 22 42 57 Martela O.F., 6
12 23 29 25 Satquote British Defender, 10
13 02 53 49 Charles Jourdan, 7
13 04 40 30 Fazisi, 9
13 05 11 08 Gatorade, 11
13 10 50 24 NCB Ireland, 13
13 14 27 42 Belmont Finland II, 12
14 14 17 58 Liverpool Enterprise, 15
14 20 40 06 Union Bank of Finland, 14

4. Leg Auckland - Punta del Este, 6,200 miles
Combined leg 1 + 2 + 3 + 4
22 20 41 53 Steinlager 2, 1
22 21 03 11 Fisher & Paykel, 3
23 09 00 11 Rothmans, 4
23 10 30 32 Merit *, 2
23 14 18 05 Charles Jourdan *, 5
23 18 12 29 Union Bank of Finland *, 11
24 17 28 29 Gatorade, 8
24 18 12 47 The Card, 6
24 23 31 22 NCB Ireland, 12
25 00 45 54 Belmont Finland II, 13
25 01 17 31 Fortuna Extra Lights, 7
25 01 31 12 Satquote British Defender, 9
25 07 01 15 Fazisi, 10
26 02 56 09 Liverpool Enterprise, 15
DNF Martela O.F. Lost her keel 250 miles from Punta del Este*
*Elapsed time modified by international jury

5. Leg Punta del Este - Fort Lauderdale, USA, 5.450 miles
Combined leg 1 + 2 + 3 + 4 + 5
22 16 41 11 Steinlager 2, 1
22 17 15 41 Fisher & Paykel, 2
22 21 33 04 Rothmans, 4
23 10 52 24 Merit, 3
23 15 24 19 The Card, 5
23 18 49 47 British Satquote Defender, 8
24 00 33 43 Union Bank of Finland, 10
24 03 24 54 NCB Ireland, 12

24 04 23 00 Belmont Finland II, 13
24 05 03 34 Gatorade, 9
24 10 07 15 Fortuna Extra Lights, 7
24 11 34 24 Charles Jourdan, 6
25 01 57 37 Fazisi, 11
26 01 36 30 Liverpool Enterprise, 14
D N C Martela O.F.

6. Leg Fort Lauderdale - Southampton, 3.837 miles
17 00 23 15 Steinlager 2
17 00 59 40 Fisher & Paykel
17 02 43 45 Merit
17 12 50 03 Rothmans (1)
17 19 07 25 The Card
17 20 35 27 Belmont Finland II
17 21 44 56 Fortuna Extra Light
18 04 21 09 Fazisi
18 06 08 57 Union Bank of Finland
18 13 29 10 NCB Ireland
18 15 44 49 Gatorade (2)
18 16 01 34 Charles Jourdan
19 03 45 24 Liverpool Enterprise
23 16 26 24 Satquote British Defender (3)

(1) Broken diagonal stay. Returned to USA for repair.
(2) Broken spreader. Returned to USA for repair.
(3) Broke the mast. Continued 2,700 miles under jury rig.

**TOTAL Leg 1-6 WHITBREAD ROUND THE WORLD RACE
1989/89** 32.932 miles
128 09 40 30 Steinlager 2
129 21 18 22 Fisher & Paykel
130 10 10 14 Merit *
131 04 54 23 Rothmans
135 07 15 43 The Card
136 15 14 51 Charles Jourdan *
137 08 14 11 Fortuna Extra Light
138 14 30 12 Gatorade *
138 16 38 12 Union Bank of Finland *
139 04 31 13 Belmont Finland II
139 09 01 04 Fazisi
139 19 22 38 NCB Ireland
143 12 42 23 Satquote British Defender
151 04 52 22 Liverpool Enterprise
D N F Martela
*Elapsed time modified by international jury.

*1989/90 Whitbread Round the World Race
Trophy for Class 'A' Maxis.*

Boat Name	Owner/ Captain	Registry	Sail No.	Designer	Builder	Year	IOR	LOA	LWL	Beam
ICAYA										
Boomerang	George S. Coumantaros/ Jeffry Neuberth	U.S.A.	US 37000	German Frers	Robert E. Derecktor	1984	70.00'	24.56m 80.5'	20.20m 66.3'	6.00m 19.7'
Congere VI	Bevin D. Koeppel	U.S.A.	US 6	German Frers	Merrifield-Roberts, Inc.	1987	69.93'	23.49m 77.07'	19.20m 63.0'	5.88m 19.3'
Drumbeat	Alan Bond	Australia	KA R2	David Pedrick	Peter Milner	1989	70.04'	25.06m 82.22'	20.4m 66.93'	6.13m 20.11'
Emeraude	Jacques Dewailly/ Mick Harvey	France	F 9333	German Frers	Eric Goetz	1989	70.05'	24.25m 79.6'	19.7m 64.6'	6.10m 20.0'
Hispania	Spanish Navy/ Juan Carlos Rodriguez-Toubes	Spain	E 10000	Bruce Farr	Astilleros Barracuda	1988	70.00'	24.48m 80.3'	19.68m 64.6'	6.07m 19.9'
Il Moro di Venezia III	Raul Gardini * Paul Cayard	Italy	I 11111	German Frers	S.A.I. Ambrosini	1987	70.05'	24.275m 79.6'	20.0m 65.6'	6.24m 20.5'
Inspiration	Herbert Dahm/ Beilken	Germany	G 1913	Ron Holland	Jongert	1985	60.18'	22.08m 72.4'	18.30m 60.1'	5.77m 18.9'
Kialoa V	John B. Kilroy	U.S.A.	US 13131	German Frers	Mefasa	1986	70.05'	24.00m 78.7'	19.6m 64.3'	5.977m 19.6'
Longobarda	Gianni Varasi/ Paolo Cappoli & Lorenzo Bortolotti	Italy	I 11611	Bruce Farr	S.A.I. Ambrosini	1989	70.00'	24.32m 79.8'	19.86m 65.2'	6.09m 20.0'
Matador	William I Koch/ Peter Grubb	U.S.A.	US 33955	German Frers	Huisman	1983	70.01'	24.72m 81.1'	21.4m 70.07'	6.03m 19.8'
Milene V	Albert Mirlesse/ Jean Guillen	England	K 904	Giles Vaton	Construction Mecanique de Normandie	1985	70.05'	24.48m 80.3'	19.75m 64.8'	6.20m 20.3'
Mistress Quickly	William V. Whitehouse-Vaux/ George Chew	Bermuda	KB 41	Ben Lexcen	Halverson & Gowland	1975	61.25'	22.07m 73'	20.3m 66.6'	4.58m 15.0'
Ondine VII	Huey Long/ Joe Jones	England	K 1015	German Frers	W.A. Souter LTD.	1986	70.04'	24.5m 80.38'	20.4m 67.0'	5.98m 19.62'
Sovereign	Bernard Lewis * David Kellet	Australia	KA 130	David Pedrick	Lewiac Pty.Ltd.	1986	70.00'	25.38m. 83.3'	21.64m 71.0'	6.09m 20.0'
Windward Passage II	Rod Muir * John McClure	Australia	KA 1988	German Frers	McConaghy/ SP Systems	1988	70.05'	24.342m 79.9'	19.7m 64.6'	6.10m 20.0'
WRTWR	**Owner/ Skipper**									
Belmont Finland II	Harry Harkimo	Finland	L 8009	Bruce Farr	Decision SA-Morges	1985	70.00'	24.5m 80.38'	19.16m 62.86'	5.63m 18.47'
British Satquote Defender	Klaus Hebben/ Cdr. Colin Watkins	England	K 303	Martin Francis & Jacques Fauroux	Green Marine	1989	69.99'	24.20m 79.42'	21.03m 69.00'	5.75m 18.83'
Charles Jourdan	Sandro Buzzi/ Alain Gabbay	France	F 8992	Guy Ribadeau Dumas	Nordhal Mabire/ Mag	1989	69.5'	22.00m 72.18'	20.40m 66.9'	5.29m 17.36'
Fazisi	Skip Novak	U.S.S.R.	SR 1989	Design-Group VTK, Poti	Poti Shipbuilding Plant	1989	70.00'	25.23m 82.75'	21.37m 70.92'	5.80m 19.0'
Fisher & Paykel	Gianni Varasi, new owner 1990 Grant Dalton	New Zealand	KZ-400	Bruce Farr	Marten Marine Industries Ltd.	1988	69.97'	24.98m 81.96'	19.90m 65.29'	5.66m 18.57'
Fortuna Extra Lights	Jan Santana Fuster & Javier de la Gandara Alonso	Spain	E 1992	Javier Visiers Rodriguez	Visiers de la Rocha-Mefasa Shipyards	1988	69.14'	23.55m 77.26'	18.48m 60.63'	5.80m 19.03'
Gatorade	Giorgio Falck	Italy	I-11441	Bruce Farr	Digby Taylor, New Zealand	1985	70.00'	24.40m 80.00'	19.45m 63.75'	5.54m 18.17'
Liverpool Enterprise	Bob Salmon	England	K-696	Bruce Farr	RTW Yachts, Inc.	1984	69.5'	24.32m 79.83'	19.25m 63.17'	5.74m 18.83'
Martela O.F.	Markku Wiikeri	Finland	L 9000	German Frers	Baltic Yachts	1989	70.05'	24.582m 80.65'	20.00m 65.6'	5.92m 19.42'
Merit	Pierre Fehmann	Switzerland	Z-3333	Bruce Farr	Decision SA - Morges	1988	70.00'	24.57m 80.61'	19.68m 64.57'	5.45m 17.88'
NCB Ireland	Joe English	Ireland	IR-1992	Ron Holland	Killian Bushe & Rob Lipsett	1988	70.00'	24.25m 80.83'	20.26m 66.42'	6.09m 20.0'
Rothmans	Lawrie Smith	England	K 100	Robert Humphreys	Paragon Composites Ltd.	1989	70.00'	24.54m 81.00'	20.14m 66.0'	5.98m 19.62'
Steinlager 2	Peter Blake, MBE	New Zealand	KZ-2	Bruce Farr	Southern Pacific Boatyard, Ltd.	1989	70.05'	25.49m 83.63'	20.29m 66.57'	5.76m 18.9'
The Card	Ted Turner, Jr., new owner 1990 John Baker/ Roger Nilson	Sweden	42624	Bruce Farr	Eric Goetz	1988	70.00'	24.03m 78.84'	19.32m 63.39'	5.63m 18.47'
Union Bank of Finland	Ludde Ingvall	Finland	L 8008	Michel Joubert & Bernard Nivelt	Laivateollisuus OY	1988	70.00'	25.20m 82.67'	20.90m 68.58'	5.80m 19.03'

Draft	Displacement	Sail loft	Sail Area Main	Head	Spinnaker	Mast/ Rig Type	Winches	Constr. Material	Constr. Method	Remarks
3.85m 12.6'	35,000kg 77,160lbs	North	156.39m 1,683 sq.ft.	215.94m 2,324 sq.ft.	478.01m 5,145 sq.ft.	Hall Spar/ Masthead	Barient	Aluminum 5083	Welded	
3.48m 13.06'	40,000/ 19,640kg 88,183/ 43,298lbs	North	144.09m 1,551 sq.ft.	221.62m 2,386 sq.ft.	480.51m 5,172 sq.ft.	Masthead	Barient	Aluminum	Welded	
4.34m 14.24'	37,200kg 82,012lbs	North, Sydney	269.82m 2,904 sq.ft.	180.59m 1,944 sq.ft.	399.76m 4,303 sq.ft.	Fractional	Lewmar	Composite	Vacuum Bagged	
4.20m 13.8'	35,000/ 22,750kg 77,160/ 50,154lbs	North	190.85m 2,054 sq.ft.	173.69m 1,870 sq.ft.	384.47m 4,139 sq.ft.	Sparcraft/ Fractional	Barient	Carbon Fibre/ Nomex Honeycombe Core	Wet laminate/ Resin content controlled by machine	
4.33m 14.2'	38,198kg 84,211lbs	Diamond/ North	169m 1,819 sq.ft.	207m 2,228 sq.ft.	382m 4,112 sq.ft.	Sparcraft	Barient	Composite	Vacuum Bagged	
4.15m 13.6'	35,600kg 78,483lbs	North	192.89m 2,076 sq.ft.	178.86m 1,925 sq.ft.	395.92m 4,262 sq.ft.	Fractional	Barient	Aluminum	Welded	*Bought by Mr. Gatti 1990, named Vanitas
3.76m 12.3'	38,000kg 83,774lbs	Beilken	126m 1,356 sq.ft.	220m 2,368 sq.ft.	450m 4,844 sq.ft.	Rondal/ Masthead	Lewmar	Aluminum	Welded	
4.06m 13.3'	37,820/ 21,247kg 83,377/ 46,841lbs	North	148.62m 1,600 sq.ft.	217.03m 2,336 sq.ft.	480.41m 5,171 sq.ft.	Masthead	Lewmar	Aluminum	Welded	
4.31m 14.14'	37,808kg 83,351lbs	North Italy	197m 2,121 sq.ft.	181m 1,948 sq.ft.	335m 3,606 sq.ft.	Sparcraft/ Fractional	Barient	Composite Kevlar + Carbon	Vacuum Bagged	
4.14m 13.6'	37,500kg 82,672lbs	Sobstad Halsey North	147.69m 1,590 sq.ft.	206.41m 2,222 sq.ft.	456.91m 4,918 sq.ft.	Masthead	Lewmar	Aluminum 5083	Welded	
4.20m 13.8'	33,490kg 73,832lbs	North	176.2m 1,897 sq.ft.	163.9m 1,764 sq.ft.	362.7m 3,904 sq.ft.	Sparcraft/ Fractional	Lewmar	Epoxy Impregnated GRP	Vacuum Bagged	
3.78m 12.4'	29,839kg 65,782lbs	Hood Sobstad North	92.4m 995 sq.ft.	161.2m 1,736 sq.ft.	356.9m 3,842 sq.ft.	Masthead	Barient	Aluminum	Welded	
4.14m 13.58'	37,649 / 20,094 kg 83,000 / 44,300 lbs	Hasley Sobstad Doyle	152.83m 1,645 sq.ft.	225.24m 2,425 sq.ft.	498.60m 5,367 sq.ft.	Masthead	Barient	Composite	Vacuum Bagged	
4.41m 14.6'	34.475/ 19,050 kg 76,000/ 42,000lbs	Hood North	189.57m 2,041 sq.ft.	214.86m 2,313 sq.ft.	475.61m 5,120 sq.ft.	Sparcraft/ Masthead	Lewmar	Aluminum	Welded	*Bought by Victor Fargo 1989
3.95m 13'	38,100kg 83,995lbs	Fraser Sails	178.54m 1,922 sq.ft.	176.41m 1,899 sq.ft.	390.49m 4,203 sq.ft.	Whale Spars/Fractional	Lewmar	Composite	Vacuum Bagged	*Bought by Raul Gardini 1989
4.08m 13.39'	28,917kg 63,750lbs	WB-Sails	180m 1,938 sq.ft.	157m 1.690 sq.ft.	289m 3,111 sq.ft.	Marechal/ Fractional	Barborossa	FRP Composite	Vacuum Bagged	
3.81m 12.5'	30,545kg 67,339lbs	Sobstad/ Hood	127.4m 1,371 sq.ft.	154.2m 1,659 sq.ft.	210m 2,260 sq.ft.	Proctor/ Fractional	Lewmar	Composite	Vacuum Bagged	
3.02m 9.84'	18,300kg 40,344lbs	North/ Voiles Systeme	145m 1,561 sq.ft.	105m 1,130 sq.ft.	250m 2,691'	Marechal/ Fractional	Harken/ Barbarossa	Prepeg Carbon	Vacuum Bagged	
3.20m 10.5'	25,500/ 10,000kg 56,217/ 22,046lbs	North	155m 1,668 sq.ft.	105m 1,130 sq.ft.	210m 2,261 sq.ft.	Sparecraft/ Fractional	Barient	Aluminum	Welded	
3.85m 12.63'	31,914kg 70,357lbs	North	125m 1,346 sq.ft.	176m 1,895sq.ft.	325m 3,498 sq.ft.	Mizzen Staysail * Masthead Ketch	Lewmar	FRP Composite	Vacuum Bagged	*Mizzen Staysail 166m/ 1,787sq.ft.
4.05m 13.33'	23,420kg 51,631lbs	Toni Tió Velas Doyle	140m 1,507 sq.ft.	136m 1,464sq.ft.	290m 3,122 sq.ft.	Fractional	Lewmar	Composite	Vacuum Bagged	
3.81m 12.5'	27,213kg 59,993lbs	Sobstad	174m 1,873 sq.ft.	163m 1,755 sq.ft.	300m 3,229 sq.ft.	Marechal/ Fractional	Barient/ Barbarossa	FRP Composite	Vacuum Bagged	
3.75m 12.33'	30,332kg 66,869lbs	Mix/ North	139m 1,496 sq.ft.	186m 2,002 sq.ft.	343m 3,692 sq.ft.	Rondal/ Masthead	Lewmar	FRP Composite	Vacuum Bagged	
3.9m 12.75'	29,730kg /16,513kg 65,400lbs /36,404lbs	Hood Doyle WB-Sails	173.78m 1,871 sq.ft.	162.53m 1,750 sq.ft.	359.78m 3,873 sq.ft.	Sparcraft/ Fractional	Lewmar	Composite	Vacuum Bagged	
3.93m 12.89'	32,649kg 71,978lbs	North	193m 2,078 sq.ft.	160m 1,722 sq.ft.	296m 3,186 sq.ft.	Alusuisse SA Favre Structure/ Fractional	Lewmar	FRP Composite	Vacuum Bagged	
3.96m 13'	31,564kg 69,440lbs	North, Canada Sobstad	199m 2,142 sq.ft.	174m 1,873 sq.ft.	372m 4,004 sq.ft.	Fractional	Lewmar	Composite	Vacuum Bagged	
3.82m 12.53'	29,000kg 63,933lbs	North	179.2m 1,930 sq.ft.	161m 1,733 sq.ft.	356.4m 3,836 sq.ft.	Sparcraft/ Fractional	Lewmar	Composite	Vacuum Bagged	
3.99m 13.09'	35,177kg 77,551lbs	North	163m 1,755 sq.ft.	158m 1,701 sq.ft.	291m 3,132 sq.ft.	Mizzen Staysail * Fractional Ketch	Barient	FRP Composite	Vacuum Bagged	*Mizzen Staysail 196m/ 2,110 sq.ft.
4.13m 13.55'	30,012kg 66,164lbs	North	123m 1,324 sq.ft.	174m 1,873 sq.ft.	321m 3,455 sq.ft.	Mizzen Staysail * Masthead Ketch	Lewmar	FRP Composite	Vacuum Bagged	*Mizzen Staysail 170m/ 1,830 sq.ft.
3.9m 12.75'	29,222/ 13,500kg 64,288/ 29,762lbs	North	205m 2,207 sq.ft.	165m 1,776 sq.ft.	365m 3,929 sq.ft.	Nokia Cable/ Aluminum unit/ Fractional	Lewmar	Deck: Composite Hull: Aluminum	Vacuum Bagged Welded	

Comparative Chart of Maxi Statistics

Steinlager 2 en route to the finish line at Southampton. Skipper Peter Blake and crew celebrate their victory with champagne.